*Lapsed Agn...*

# Lapsed Agnostic

## JOHN WATERS

continuum

**Continuum UK**
The Tower Building, 11 York Road, London SE1 7NX

**Continuum US**
80 Maiden Lane, Suite 704, New York, NY 10038

www.continuumbooks.com

First published 2008

*British Library Cataloguing-in-Publication Data*
A catalogue record for this book is available from the British Library.

ISBN 0-8264-9146-4

Typeset by Kenneth Burnley, Wirral, Cheshire
Printed and bound by MPG Books Ltd, Bodmin, Cornwall

# Contents

# — 1 —

# The Tunnel of Trees

My first notion of my relationship with God was based on the idea of a child with a toy. I was God's doll, or, more correctly, one of God's millions of dolls. He played with me when it suited Him. Sometimes He favoured me, and sometimes He was cruel or careless or arbitrary. Sometimes I felt like I'd been forgotten; occasionally that I was, like the Velveteen Rabbit or the teddy bear I inherited from my older sister, a favourite toy. And yet, I simultaneously had the idea that God loomed large over me, watching my every move. It was as though He had set up a clockwork doll's house, and was constantly patrolling around it: adjusting, teasing, rewinding, and displaying either pleasure or irritation with what He observed.

I don't know where this idea came from, but I'm pretty sure it pre-existed the catechism we studied so exhaustively for Confirmation. This tiny but terrifying red-covered book told us that God, the Creator and Sovereign Lord of heaven and earth and of all things, would reward the good and punish the wicked. It told us that God was everywhere but that He manifested His glory only in heaven, where His company was enjoyed by the blessed. God had no beginning and would have no end. He had no body and could not been seen by us. Nevertheless, He could see us and watched over us constantly. He knew all things, even our most secret thoughts and actions, and would judge us accordingly. He was all powerful, and could do anything He put His mind to. He had made the world out of nothing for His own glory, to demonstrate His power and wisdom and, to what seemed to be a significantly lesser extent, for man's use and benefit.

God, therefore, was something of an egomaniac: a distant, hyper-active, judgemental, vindictive, compulsive-obsessive, who needed constant attention and flattery or He would exact some terrible vengeance. We didn't have these terms or perspectives to hand at the time, but that, in retrospect, was what I secretly felt about God but wouldn't dare even begin to frame as thoughts.

Despite having no body, God managed to have a long beard, and was dressed in a kind of long white vestment-type garment. He was bald on top but had long hair down his back and shoulders. He wore sandals, without socks. I'm not sure where the sandals came from, because God usually manifested Himself only from the waist up, the lower half of His body being suffused in fluffy white clouds. I think the baldness was a way of distinguishing Him from Jesus, whose hair, though also long, was dark brown and curly and perfectly matched a rich, luxuriant beard. This was the figure from the Sacred Heart pictures which hung in almost every Irish living room and, with pictures of the pope and John Fitzgerald Kennedy on either side, providing an unintended reminder of the good thief and the bad thief on Calvary. I remember becoming confused and disoriented once watching a movie depicting the passion of Christ, which had a balding actor playing Jesus. I knew from my catechism that God comprised three Divine Persons – Father, Son and Holy Ghost – who together made one God, but still I couldn't cope with the balding Jesus. God the Father was losing His hair, but it was, I sensed, a little early in the life of the Redeemer for hereditary hair loss to be manifesting.

I think these rather reductionist ideas were pretty much my own conception, based on innumerable cultural messages coming at me from all directions. Nobody actually described God to me in these terms, but the picture grew with the accumulation of images and information I absorbed as I went along.

The idea of God as Father must have contributed certain elements of this picture, but it also added to the confusion. My own father was, in a sense, distant, somewhat severe, yet sometimes mischievous and fun loving. However, he had short hair and no beard and wouldn't wear sandals to save his soul. He also wore glasses, which God, being all seeing, did not. Nevertheless, I gathered that, notwithstanding his need to be 'sucked up to', God was my Protector, and, although given to moods and grumpiness, was on the whole a decent sort and, most importantly, in my corner for as long as I remained 'good'. For all its crudity, this concept of God was extremely useful and carried within it the vague beginnings of some fairly complex ideas, such as the idea of dependence, of free will and even of original sin.

These ideas of God suffused my childhood. I was, on the surface at least, a devout child. I said my prayers, although I never quite grasped what prayer was supposed to be about. Like everyone else around me, I went to confession, mass and communion. But I had, I would say, an added layer of piety which resulted from my father's rather exaggerated religiosity. The nature of my father's faith was always inscrutable to me. People talk patronizingly nowadays about the 'simple faith' of the people of the Ireland which has, in the course of a generation, passed into history. But there was nothing simple about my father. Though uneducated in any formal sense, he was a very smart and thoughtful man who left behind him a small library of books embracing Euclid, Dickens and Shakespeare. The truth is that I haven't the faintest idea about what he believed as regards the big questions of life. He had an incontrovertible appearance of devoutness, but I know too much from looking out through the eyeholes in my own skull to read anything of this at face value.

My mother was, and remains, a devout Catholic, but her practice of the faith always appeared more, in a sense, normal than my father's. I mean normal more in a historical sense, in the sense of the entire flow of time down all the years I can remember. My mother's approach seemed, and seems, more balanced somehow. My father's practice had about it an element of intensity that both marked it out and, by a strange paradox, seemed to mirror the mood of the time, in much the same way that a great musician can capture the mood of the everyday.

My father was almost a generation older than my mother, and so was rooted in an era that was overwhelmingly defined, in the almost immediate past, by the Great Famine, and, in his teens, by the Easter Uprising, the War of Independence and the bloody Civil War. The worst of these calamities was the Famine of the 1840s, which left at least one million Irish people dead and another two million scattered around the globe. Simply by virtue of its existence and remit in a society with no other indigenous means of self-organization, the Catholic Church was lumbered with responsibility for creating cohesion and providing a moral and social framework to, in effect, ensure that Ireland could contrive to avoid such a calamity in the future. It was to become perhaps its most disadvantageous characteristic that, in the necessary moral reconstruction that occurred as a consequence of these events, the Catholic Church became a supreme player, a sort of surrogate moral government which assumed responsibility for social as well as for moral and spiritual affairs.

As far as I am able to divine, I was conceived on my father's fiftieth birthday, and I know almost nothing of what kind of man he was before then. Occasionally I would meet men who knew him well when he was younger, and they would half-tell me stories about dances and motorbikes. But this became for me no more than the speculative building of a legend. I suspect my father reinvented his personality when he had children, as a lot of men seemed to do in those days, so as to present to us an unambiguous model of uprightness. But if his religiosity was a part of this reinvention, it was without doubt founded on something much deeper than a desire for respectability. I have no doubt that not only was his faith sincerely felt but it was something he thought about a great deal. He never talked about it, other than in occasional admonitions cast in our, his children's direction, usually amounting to the assertion that we had no religion. We were 'pagans', he would say. Often these observations would be presented as oblique parables constructed around some event or individual in the town, in which the phenomenon of 'paganism' was especially conspicuous. The implication of what was really half a joke centred on the notion of our dissolution. We were not merely unbelievers, but uncivilized with it.

It strikes me now that my father was, if not a typical man of his time, in some odd way emblematic of the totality of the culture in that now seemingly far-off era. He had inherited a faith which, if he questioned it at all, he questioned it in the privacy of his own thoughts. It was a faith that sustained him, that provided him with an identity, that motivated him through a life of relative poverty and considerable hardship. In this he was a product of post-Famine Ireland who had lived slightly beyond his time. It wasn't that he 'believed' in God: he simply took it for granted that God existed. The idea of questioning the existence of God would for him have been as unthinkable as questioning the existence of the America to which most of his family had disappeared. I don't know how literally he took the prevailing images of God, but he certainly did or said nothing to correct the somewhat colourful and contradictory images running riot around my brain. He took no interest in what they taught me at school, but merely assumed that I knew the same things that he knew and believed them just as absolutely.

When I think back to the heyday of Irish Catholicism, a period which seems to overlap with the early part of my life, I think of it as reflecting the complexity of my father's life and temperament. An accusation that is levelled at the Catholicism of the Ireland into which my generation was born is that it was rooted in aspirations to respectability. There is a caricature of those times which portrays an ostentatious piety designed, first of all, to convey itself to an imagined audience, a devotion exaggerated for show. Nothing could have been further from my father's mind. You had only to look at his ragged coat to know that he had no desire whatever to be respectable in the conventional sense of the word. Indeed, he despised 'respectable' society and increasingly became alienated from a Catholic clergy which he perceived to be pandering to this respectability. Though extremely devout, he couldn't have cared less what anyone thought of him. I sometimes wonder if this lack of concern for an audience was not in itself part of a more calculated and complex demonstration, but this kind of scepticism I find unproductive and more than a little unworthy. If it looks like a duck and walks like a duck and quacks like a duck, the chances are it's not a partridge in a pear tree.

Although he visited the church nearly every evening of his working life, he did not do so for purposes of ostentation or conformity. I accompanied him on numerous occasions and most of the time we met almost nobody. At Sunday mass, he would go to the same place every week – the space beside the confessional box in the left-hand aisle, about halfway down. I don't know why he liked this particular space, but I fancy it was because it placed him approximately halfway between the 'respectable' people in the conventional pews and the 'cornerboy' fraternity congregating just inside the door. (All cornerboys were pagans, though not all pagans were cornerboys.)

I think he would have been too self-conscious to go into a conventional pew. The position he chose, because it had no seat in front, gave him more room to spread himself out. He never sat down or stood up, but knelt continuously with one knee on his cap, not to protect his trousers but presumably to soften the strain on his knee. He never took any part in the liturgy, never acknowledged proceedings in any way, but simply said the rosary to himself continuously during mass. As the time passed, he slumped forward until he was virtually prostrate on the floor, his head bowed down, like a bishop being consecrated, but oblivious to everyone around him. For me, he conveyed at all times a sense, not of practised belief, still less of preserving an outward appearance, but of an existence lived in the utter conviction of another reality. His whole life was like this, and in many ways ours became so too, as an inevitable consequence of his personality and outlook. He seemed to need nothing except his work, sleep, three meals a day, nightly prayers, and the newspaper. He seemed to carry with him the sense of Catholicism as an essential element of survival, as a tool for dealing with a hard and unrelenting reality. It was as though he had breathed in the entire recent history of Ireland and was recreated in its image.

My father lived for nearly 85 years in this world but for as much of his life as I consciously knew him (roughly the final third) he seemed to belong to the next. I do not believe that his faith had anything to do with fear of death. I never once observed my father manifest fear of anything. Rather, his belief in God and his observance of the Catholic faith were both a reasoned response to the exigencies of a tough and unrelenting reality, and a source of comfort and motivation in a life characterized by monotonous and continuous hard work. He worked roughly fifteen hours a day, six days a week, until he was well into his seventies. He had no social life other than communication with the people he met in the course of his working day, though, as I have written elsewhere, this was intense and rewarding for him. His asceticism, which went beyond the monkish, seemed to be rooted in a view of reality that included the afterlife as an intrinsic part of that reality. Towards the end of his life he had accumulated a degree of financial security, mainly through his ownership of several small farms. But this did little to alter our actual circumstances or to render him more susceptible to materialism. Rather it was an additional expression of the virtue that he had apparently enforced upon himself, the objective evidence of his industry. This, at least, was part of the story – there was another, more ambiguous, element to his asceticism which I have inherited and which I will come to later.

Although at the upper level, Irish society of the 1960s and early 1970s retained elements of a materialist hierarchy, the majority of people defined themselves, not on the basis of what they had, but on what they were and what they did. In those days, to be described as a 'good worker' was close to the highest compliment a man could be paid. Industry, thrift and adherence to duty were badges of especial honour in a society which had few material resources to share around. Hard work was, of course, essential if a man was to house, feed and clothe his family, but it was also a way of displaying virtue and therefore of acquiring an acceptable, admirable identity. And this sense of virtue, while in turn motivated by a man's desire to provide for his dependants, was also rooted in a cultural sense of goodness that had its roots in Christian notions of the Good Man. To work hard was to be on God's team, to enjoy a constant sense of fulfilment on the basis of being able to compare oneself favourably with the less industrious, with the 'cornerboys' and 'bowsies' who took both work and church less seriously. To be idle, for my father, was to feel bad. He never took days off, or went on holidays, or even trips of any kind that were not necessitated by some practical exigency such as a medical check-up or a consultation with his lawyer. He was not a 'Pioneer'; that is, he had not sworn off drink completely, but he rarely drank other than, as he used to pointedly observe, 'for medicinal purposes'. At the back of this constant pursuit of a personal sense of virtue there appeared to be a belief that the human being was prone to temptation and mischief if not preoccupied with useful endeavour, though this dark side of the human condition became nullified in the personality of someone who was, in the almost reverential phrase of the time, 'a great worker', and therefore someone who appeared to have eliminated all possibility of leisure or frivolity from his life. I can say with certainty, based on various things that my father said during my childhood, that he would not have entertained any concept of a 'deserving poor', but regarded such poverty as evidence of moral failing, rectifiable only by hard work. To his mind, work and religious observance seemed to go hand in hand. He disdained all trappings of earthly indulgence, and, although he was a witty and mischievous man, would use words like 'fun', 'conceit' and 'pleasure' as disapproving epithets to describe those of more worldly polarity. In all this he seemed to embody the cultural value system of a post-Famine Ireland, in which the most abundant resources were piety, labour and faith.

With the best will in the world, this model of Catholicism could hope to offer nothing to the generations born after the middle of the twentieth century. The world was changing, of course, making inevitable the failure of the existing brand of Irish Catholicism to catch fire with the first generations to grow up in Ireland, post-independence, post-war and, eventually, post the notion of frugal comfort, as de Valera described the kind of lifestyle my father and his generation sought to lead. Young Irish people were becoming better educated, slightly more prosperous, but, more importantly, more exposed to the burgeoning popular culture of other Western societies, especially the United Kingdom and the United States. The nature of work, of daily activity, was changing too. My father's generation had, in a particular sense, been masters of its own economic destiny. The jobs men of this era did were mostly humble in terms of both status and income, but they had the saving grace of allowing men to be something. My father, as mailcar driver, had a status, but also a visible role in society. He did things that mattered and could be observed by others. He had tangible skills. Most men of the time were in similar situations. They were carpenters, painters, shoemakers, electricians, who by virtue of their individual skills acquired confidence and, more importantly, authority, based on the idea that they, in a sense, owned their own capacities to feed their families. When I was a child, most men were like this. Nowadays, both men and women are breadwinners, but mostly they operate in a completely different climate. They work in offices or factories, where the ability to continue earning is predicated less on an individual's own skill base than on the whim of the employer. There has, therefore, been a diminution of the general capacity of the individual to convey a sense of authority on the basis of having acquired and pursued a useful function. Authority now resides with State institutions and their officials. It is bureaucratic and anonymous and, for these reasons, a target of vague but quite generalized resentment. Moreover, because the initiation of much of the activity in the Irish economy has occurred outside the society, there is a heightened sense of dependency which further alienates people from the concept of authority. Combined with the aftershocks of a series of revelations concerning the betrayal of authority figures in various institutions, most notably the Catholic Church, the effect of this has been to heighten in the collective imagination a resentment towards, and a resistance to, all forms of authority.

These factors, together with the intrinsic weakness of the existing model of Catholicism, served to render the demise of Catholicism a foregone conclusion. To begin with, there was little conscious memory of the events in which the existing model of Catholicism was so firmly rooted. The Great Famine was not talked about. You might expect an event with such a cataclysmic effect on the society it had ravaged to loom very large in the culture, but the opposite was the case. One school of thought on the subject of this silence would put it down to the forgetting that afflicts post-colonial societies concerning what has been a tremendous source of shame. Occupation, and the radical interference that accompanies it, provokes at a surface level a consciousness that can lead to rebellion. But deeper down it invites amnesia. To be colonized is to be proved worthless in your own eyes. At various levels of the colonized society, there is a high degree of acceptance of the message of the colonizer – that the native society is, left alone, capable of nothing but savagery, that its indigenous culture is worthless, and that its only hope of redemption resides in imitation of the conqueror. Since the Famine of the 1840s was the most traumatic event in the bloody history of Ireland's relationship with England, it became, in a sense, an emblem of shame, firstly because it served as a reminder of humiliation, but also because, having reduced the Irish people to their most desperate state, it inevitably raised the most profound questions as to the morality of having survived it at all. What did any individual, any family, have to do to stay alive when so many others were dead and gone? What trade-offs? What crimes? What compromises? What dishonour? The silence arising from the evasion of these questions caused the Famine to be, if not forgotten, certainly pushed into the recesses of the memory, and talked about less and less.

There was also, as often occurs in such societies, a consolidation by the middle classes around the fiction of normality. Having bought the colonizer's description of reality, hook, line and sinker, those with something to lose moved to create a subtly different version of reality. There had been no colonization, no real quarrel with England, but simply outbreaks of bother, caused mainly by disgruntled elements within. This led to the emergence of euphemistic phrases like 'the Troubles' to describe the extended period of conflict that followed the abortive rising of 1916 – later to be appended also to the outbreak of conflict in the north of the country after the putting down of the civil rights movement in 1969.

The problem for the Catholic Church in all this was that it took the wrong side. Having long been a rebel church on the side of the people during the most traumatic of times, it moved after independence to establish itself as a central element of the new 'respectable' Ireland that was seeking to construct a self-sustaining society and re-write the problematic bits of its past history. The Church became associated with nationalism and with a superficially nationalistic version of history, but this was an account of past events that failed to acknowledge the deeper trauma that had been inflicted and, more significantly, was silent on the nature of the remedies that had been put in place by the Church itself. The Church became, then, a mouthpiece of the normalizing tendency and occasionally a proponent of crude and largely rhetorical brands of nationalism. Society not only became increasingly deprived of the most basic insights into its own psychological condition, but also lost sight of why Irish Catholicism had evolved in the way it had. I think this is partly why people like my father practised a form of the faith which, though conducted on the premises provided by the Church, sought to make a connection with something else, as though bypassing the gombeen nature of what the Church had become.

And if the Church had failed to hold the imaginations of people like my father, what hope could it have of holding on to the generations reared on television, rock 'n' roll and the sexual revolution?

For a while I tried to emulate my father's religiosity but without much success. He was a hard act to follow, and my spirit was weak. He prayed every evening, in front of us but alone. He would first of all read prayers from a book while sitting in his armchair and then produce his rosary beads from his pocket and turn around and kneel at the chair to say the rosary. He prayed silently and never once, to the best of my memory, asked any of us to join him. I have no idea why. He also, as well as going to mass on Sundays, visited the church most evenings after work. For a time, when I was perhaps ten or eleven, I fell into the habit of going along with him. I think it was my way of currying favour with both God and my father, who often struck me as equally disapproving of me, though I have little memory now of why I felt this. I used to think my father carried his faith as a kind of accusation against the rest of us, but nevertheless he allowed us total freedom of conscience to do as we pleased when it came to religion, while letting it be known that his approval of us was inextricably bound up with our behaviour in matters of devotion. For a time I took to playing up to this. I remember many evenings, mainly dark winter ones, over what seems like several years, when I would go to meet him at the post office and accompany him to the church.

As I have said, he worked as a mailcar driver, transporting mail between the area post office which was in our home town, Castlerea, and a dozen or so sub-offices in the surrounding countryside. He finished work about seven, when he had delivered his evening mail collection to the post office. Setting out from home, I would invest myself with the personality of a fictional character from some comic or book I happened to be reading, perhaps Paul Terune, the languid private detective from the *Hornet*, and walk through the rain-sodden town to meet my informant. On the way, I would stop off at Burkes' sweetshop just over the bridge, and buy a shilling's worth of Zoo Animals. These were jelly sweets in the shapes of tigers, lions and elephants, and had a consistency which is nowadays only approximated in the comestible universe by wine gums. I would put the bag of sweets in my overcoat pocket to allow for easy access. An exchange of nods with my father would usually be the only preliminary communication between us as we set off through the glistening streets, I observing passing pedestrians for suspicious behaviour that might lead to a breakthrough in whatever was my case of the moment. Sometimes there would be a prayer service under way in the church, but usually the church was empty except for ourselves. Sometimes it might appear empty but, after a while a cough or a sibilant smattering of whispered prayerful ejaculations would betray the presence of an old woman pleading with God with a hint of desperation that always scared me rigid. Outwardly, my father and I would give the impression of a devout father and son, piously doing the Stations of the Cross. I can't speak for my father, but inwardly I was anything but devout, As though oblivious of the all-seeing God, my head would be full of plot twists and investigatory conundrums as I wrote each person I encountered into the unfolding saga in my head. Posing as a devout Catholic boy, I would in truth be on the trail of a serial murderer or on the point of discovering the hiding place of a gang of jewel thieves. As we walked around the fourteen stations, I would surreptitiously transport Zoo Animals from pocket to mouth, trying to guess the colour and shape of each one by teasing it with my tongue. Mindful of the sacred context, I allowed myself just one sweet per station.

In these years I became for my father a kind of aide-de-camp who represented him on important occasions in the town, which invariably meant funerals. Funerals in country towns were often major gatherings, for which the whole town seemed to change gear for the couple of days between the announcement and the burial. Because of his work, my father was rarely able to attend. This was his stated reason anyway, but the truth is he would have felt out of place in the social event that a funeral inevitably became. He had a preoccupation with sending mass cards to the bereaved, even people he seemed to know only slightly, and the execution of this duty fell largely to me. My father would buy the mass card and give it to me, together with a pound note for the priest. I would have to go to the canon's house, or sometimes the presbytery, depending on which cleric was most in favour with my father at the time. I would then have to attend the funeral to drop the card in the box in front of the coffin and sympathize with the family. If anyone thought it odd for a 10-year-old boy to be walking the line of bereaved relatives intoning, 'Sorry for your trouble', they gave no hint of it. I would often attend three or four funerals a week, especially at the peak season for mortality, just after Christmas.

Apart from the monumental influence of my father, my experience of Catholicism as a child was remarkably devoid of intensity. It was ever present, a daily adventure, but strangely lacking in meaning. We never absorbed anything of theology or Scripture, apart from the rote answers to the questions in our little catechism, a handful of prayers and a few woolly stories about Pharisees and tax-collectors. What was known as 'devotional literature' – a selection of Catholic periodicals of varying emphasis and quality – came into our house. I read them often, usually when I ran out of other things to read, but cannot recall any of them doing anything except confirming the general sense of religiosity conveyed by church and school.

Reflecting on it now, it strikes me that the Catholicism I grew up with impressed on me the strongest possible sense of the peripherals of Christianity but almost nothing of the core meaning. God the Father, as I have outlined, was a huge presence in our lives, as a transcendent authority figure and as the source of the earthly authority of the Church. The Blessed Virgin also loomed large, being depicted everywhere in Marian shrines. The rosary, which was said everywhere all the time, addressed both these figures in explicit terms. Jesus was referred to, of course, but in a muted way. There was a vague sense that the whole point of Christianity had something important to do with Him, but there was, too, a sense that He was subordinate to the others. He had been sent by the Father to save us. From what? From the wrath of the Father. The catechism said: 'By His passion and death Christ satisfied the justice of God, and delivered us from hell, and from the power of the devil.' It would be several decades later that a tremendous priest I met in Italy explained to me that the context in which Jesus died for me and my sins had to do, not with saving me from the wrath of the Father, but with saving me from death itself. The Resurrection, he explained, was the death of death. Jesus died not because of the rage of His Father but in order to tell me that eternity was a reality. It seemed so simple. Forty years of angst fell away in an instant.

Prayer mystified me. The idea of repeating a series of formulaic incantations until you were numb with boredom held no attraction whatsoever. My attempts at prayer were characterized by an acute knowledge of failure. I would start off well, but soon, though the words would continue to flow, my mind would wander into some reverie. In a short time I would notice and pull myself back to the words, but soon another distraction would jump up in the back of my head, saying 'Hey, think about me!' The next stage was a dismayed descent into a mood of self-criticism, as, reflecting on the dismal failure of the attempt to make contact with God, I would berate myself for my frivolity. I would grind my teeth in an attempt at concentration, focusing on the meaning of every word as though I was encountering the prayer for the first time. I would soon grow bored with this, however, and another magical thought would sneak in from the recesses of my mind. I was under no illusion that I was bad at praying, which translated as bad, full stop. And yet, all the while, I had a deeper sense of the meaninglessness of saying the same words again and again to a God who presumably knew them off by heart long ago and, anyway, since he knew all things, past, present and to come, could predict the quality of my prayer output before I started. During the rosary in church, I would amuse myself by, though not counting the Hail Marys, tuning in towards the end of each decade to predict which Hail Mary we were on. In due course I acquired a flawless expertise at this.

If you ask me today to evaluate the condition of my early faith, I would say that what I felt was a constant sense of unworthiness. I felt unclean. I felt that God must be able to see through me. I felt that there was no place I could hide from my own calculation, my own self-absorption. It's not that I would have engaged in overmuch analysis of my motives or intentions, but rather that I had a constant sense of failing some unstated test of holiness. In my bones I knew that my holiness was a matter of show, that I felt nothing of what I should have felt in the knowledge and presence of God. I often wonder if my generation's retrospective disparagement of the piety of its parents' generation is more a reaction to its own forced childhood ostentation, which expresses itself as a repudiation of the alleged falsity of its religious inheritance.

My childhood experience of what we thought of as religion comes back to me in a series of images, colours, smell and tastes, as though from a five-sensed movie reel replayable at the prompting of a thought. One such reel shows reruns of the annual Corpus Christi procession which took over the town for a day in early summer, and will forever be associated in my mind with my birthday, which falls on 28 May. The procession involved the Holy Sacrament being transported from the church to somewhere such as the fair green or the market square. The priest would carry the monstrance in which was encased the sacred Host, with four members of the men's sodality holding a canopy over him. To be the altar boy with charge of the thurible on such an occasion was a privilege indeed – to walk alongside the priest, swinging the smoking urn as the whole town came out to watch. Along the route, householders would build spectacular altars outside their houses, featuring statues of the Sacred Heart, the Blessed Virgin and the Child of Prague, bedecked with bluebells, snowdrops and lupins. It is perhaps a comment on the cultural poverty of the time, but there was nothing in the cultural or sporting calendar in those days to match the Corpus Christi procession.

Another such reel relates to my first mass as an altar boy: the suddenness of it and the fuss and the burning knot of worry beginning deep in the belly so I could hardly eat or sleep. You had no way of knowing when the call would come or what the system was or why you had been chosen or not chosen yet. It could happen at any time after you went into fourth class, maybe straight away or maybe before Christmas or maybe not until the spring and sometimes not until you went into fifth class which was a sign of something, though nobody quite knew what. A few new names were announced every month, usually on a Friday evening when the class was stowing away the art things before the final bell, and your heart skipped at least five beats and then beat like fury to catch up so you could hardly hear the names, except that something had already told you that one of them wasn't going to be you. As the brother gave out the new names you would try to work out what the system was and why some had been chosen and not others. It wasn't that they were holier, or at least it didn't seem to be, because I was near enough the holiest of all and yet was one of the last to be picked. Or it might have been to do with the size of your house or the street you lived on, except that, now and then, a name would be given out that seemed to go against this general trend. Sometimes someone would be chosen early on from a poor household, but usually it would be someone whose manner had something in it to suggest that they didn't belong in a poor house. There was a sense about it, as there was a sense in almost everything, of a moral hierarchy being observed. A more mundane theory had it that the brother got it mixed up with hurling, and this, since I was useless at hurling, would explain why I was nearly the last to be selected. But I felt sure it had to do with something much more profound, like the aggregate of a number of unspecified qualities. For me, my late selection therefore dovetailed with my own sense of my place in the moral hierarchy.

But when my turn finally came, it came out of the blue, not on a Friday for a Monday morning start but on a Tuesday for a Wednesday, because one of the sixth-class boys had moved out of town, leaving a place to be filled straight away. When I heard the brother say my name, and my name only, it was as though I had been hit from behind with a flat board. I watched the room move around me, the curious turning of heads, the brother's face slowed down to yawning speed.

'Can you be at the church at half seven?'

I heard myself say 'Yes', but the ache had already started in my belly and this moment that I'd waited for brought only dread and fear. I wondered then if joy at the realization of dreams was ever possible, or if the anticipation of something was always not merely better than the reality, but the only reality joy would ever inhabit.

For several years in my late childhood, I served as an altar boy, sang in the choir for high masses and attended all the routine devotions and celebrations, but all the while I retained my sense of a darkish, forbidding God observing my every move and thought. The two things, however, never quite merged into one: the God I recognized seemed separate somehow from the acting out of religion, which for me was largely a social ritual, and sometimes a spectacular one. To be called to serve was to bear a heavy responsibility and no little prestige. That first morning as an altar boy remains unsurpassed for stress by any other event in my life, and these include High Court actions and even the Eurovision Song Contest. There was something about carrying out the fairly simple duties that filled me with dread of making a mistake. Every team of altar boys had a captain, who ruled ruthlessly and unforgivingly over the performances of his underlings. To begin with you had to work your way up through the simple duties – ringing the church bell five minutes before mass began and ministering to the priest's requirements during the 'first wine' – the filling of the chalice before the consecration – and holding the paten under the chins of communicants in case the host slipped out of the priest's hand. After this you graduated on to the 'last wine', which occurred after communion, ringing the bell during the consecration, and maintaining the thurible during benediction, priming it with incense and ensuring that it remained alight. This required almost the confidence of a priest, as the trick resided in swinging it vigorously even during the quiet periods when nothing much was happening. To let the thurible go out was close to a hanging offence, so only veterans were trusted with this job. To hit the sanctuary bell off centre and bring a note of discordance to the consecration was regarded as a serious failure.

I remember as though it were this very morning both the emotional upheaval and the physical detail of that first morning as an altar boy: the fresh silence of the street, the scent of the sprinkling of new rain on the breeze-dried dust of late March, like the taste of a penny on the tongue. I still clearly remember the fear of the journey, in the midst of all the other fears of all the other journeys through those same streets, the excitement and the terror all wound up together in a tight ball threatening to go spinning into orbit, taking me with it. I remember leaving our house, my borrowed soutane trailing in the wet of the footpath, the walk through the still-sleeping town, running past the old women as they trudged their way to the eight o'clock mass of which they were the sole patrons, reaching the sacristy and not knowing where to go. Knowing that on other such journeys I would be better able to savour my importance but for now having to postpone all this much-anticipated joy, leaving my black coat open to reveal the swan white of the surplice over the crow black of the soutane, walking purposefully and nodding thoughtfully to the old women with a cold 'Good Morning', but for now feeling nothing but the fear and dread and unknowing.

The first few days you had nothing to do except kneel there on the deep red carpet and watch. I had never knelt on a carpet before. After the first morning the fear had disappeared, leaving only the self-importance, the pride and the leaping in the heart. On the Friday morning I was allowed to hold the priest's vestment during the consecration. On Saturday I helped with the last wine, pouring the water over the priest's fingers to wash away the blood of the Lord and make sure none was wasted or spilt. But mostly in that week I knelt with my back to the church, listening and watching. Listening to the priest unleash breakneck pleadings in Latin into the mouth of the altar, his hands held out like a boastful fisherman: 'In nomine Patris, et filii et spiritus sancti . . . acipite et bibite ex eo omnes.' I had never before heard someone speak fluently in a language that was not English. I watched the priest's mouth move through the phrases with certainty and ease, his tone or delivery never extending beyond the conversational, as though he were an interpreter nominated to speak on behalf of the tiny congregation to a presence with which they all desired to commune. In the silences I knelt with eyes closed, listening to the coughs and croaks and sneezes from the body of the church, each one echoing off every pillar and buttress, flying high up into the rafters into the light of the sun through the stained-glass images of stories I knew only vaguely but which amazed me in inverse proportion to my grasp of them. I closed my eyes in pained concentration, counting and listening, and listening and counting, trying to connect coughs to faces and sneezes to stooped backs and croaks to tightened scarves around pinched faces and trembling, whispering lips.

On the Saturday of that first week I got to walk to the belfry with the team captain and watch him tug the rope and go down with it and wait for the peal of the bell and go up with the rope and ride its pursuit of the ebbing sound and come down again harder still and up and around and down and up as if he were being pulled up to heaven. And the sound of the bell happened near and yet far away, distant as though the work of other hands and yet happening now at this moment and as it had always been, as when I sat in my school desk listening and counting the minutes until lunch, or on the riverbank watching the water ripple over the stones, inhaling the scent of the whin and the smell of bread from Dyar's bakery to the south, or in the railway station at noon watching the steam rising from the rear of a departing train, or in the bog to the east with my father, handing him up the rectangular sods of turf to build into a bank as true as a gospel, my townie's hands sore and reddened, and the bell ringing out to tell us it was time for tea. And the captain, without warning, stepped back from the rope as it followed the peal of the bell into the clouds and gestured to me to take over and, pulling up his soutane, took from his pocket a box of matches which had a single cigarette butt sandwiched between the two remaining matches inside. As he took to smoking I grabbed the swinging rope in terrified hands and pulled and waited, and when nothing happened pulled again in fright, and felt the rope shudder and then heard the bell ring, not as before but hollow and short, and then nothing but the rope swinging because in my terror I had let it go. And drawing on his cigarette, the captain muttered under his breath, 'Jesus Christ, will you pull the fuckin' thing for fuck's sake?' He pushed me aside and pulled again on the rope, long and steady in harmony with the glow of the cigarette between his lips, and then stepped back again and gestured for me to have another go. This time I followed the flow of the rope around the smooth corner of the peal and as the sound drained away I pulled again, this time evenly, and listened and felt the rope run through my hands, and listened and then pulled again, and heard the bell sound as smooth and true as if someone else was ringing it and I was standing someplace else in the town where no one knew of my presence, listening to the bell sounding its call or accusation for my ears only.

Until my late teens, I successfully passed myself off as a pious boy and youth, so much so that, when I was about to go into secondary school, I received an exploratory visit from a representative of a college in the south of the country dedicated to preparing boys for the priesthood. This was not a seminary but a boarding school to which aspirant seminarians might be sent in the hope of nurturing their burgeoning vocations. The priest, a kind of recruiting sergeant for the college, visited our house and those of at least two of my classmates, one of whom would go on to become a remarkably successful womanizer. None of us took up the challenge but, in my case, this came down to finances – the fees and additional costs of attending the college were out of reach of our family circumstances.

I remained an outwardly devout Catholic until my late teens, though the more intense immersion in religion began to wane when I started playing soccer at about the age of 12. Shortly afterwards, through the influence of various friends I became interested in pop music. This interest was ludicrously random, non-chronological and unscientific in nature: T Rex, followed by the Beatles, followed by Johnny Cash, Rory Gallagher and, eventually, Horslips. This brings us to the early 1970s, when news of the pop revolution was just beginning to hit Castlerea. We grew our hair long and, when possible, wore moderately flamboyant clothes, although this flamboyance was somewhat restricted by virtue of the penguin-like outfits we were expected to wear to school. We began to dabble with guitars and flirted with songwriting. In our heads we were the Beatles. Actually, in our hearts each one of us was John. I could barely tease out three chords on the guitar, but could play the melodeon in a rather rudimentary way. I remember one winter doing a concert in the local mental hospital, performing a few marches and come-all-yes, with a version of the Dave Edmunds hit of the time, 'I Hear You Knocking' stuck incongruously in the middle. Undoubtedly it was appalling, but nobody complained, and for us it was like a combination of Johnny Cash at San Quentin and the rooftop concert from 'Let It Be'. Such fantasies were capable of keeping our spirits afloat amidst even the most unprepossessing of realities.

I am amazed in retrospect when I consider the extent to which I and the lads I hung around with then lived completely in a fantasy world. Thoughts of what we were going to do when we left school never entered our heads. I don't think it was so much that we seriously imagined we would become famous footballers or pop stars, but that we did not wish to contemplate the reality outside the cocoon of fantasy in which we lived. We read the *NME* (the *New Musical Express*) and congregated on a Thursday night in one of the other lads' houses to watch *Top of the Pops*. (It was always 'one of the other lads' houses' because my father refused to allow a television set into the house.)

The beginning of the end of this first phase of my religious life came following the rather dismal outcome of my Leaving Certificate examination. Since I was reputed to be something of a brainbox, my parents were disappointed, to say the least, when I scraped a pass in five subjects, just enough not to fail the exam. After some robust debate, it was decided that I should repeat. I was unhappy about this, but didn't have any better ideas. Feeling both aggrieved and somewhat proud of my willingness to give it a go, I found myself within a couple of days at loggerheads with the priest who came in to teach us Christian Doctrine. The outcome of this had perhaps been rendered inevitable by virtue of the fact that an elderly neighbour would regularly regale me with tales of the bacchanalian indulgences of this particular priest – late-night rambles to the homes of chancy women, vodka bottles in the dustbin at dawn, that sort of thing.

It was all something and nothing. I was sitting beside a friend of mine, the only other boy who was repeating, who made one of his cutting remarks into my ear. I laughed, the priest saw me, asked me to share the source of my amusement with the class in general and I told him it was none of his business. One word borrowed another and I decided to leave before anyone had the pleasure of throwing me out. My parents were beside themselves but I stood my ground. I didn't grasp it there and then, but that incident was also to provide me with an alibi for my withdrawal from Catholicism. I gradually came to decide that there was no point in listening to people who were manifestly all too human when it came to the things they were, as it seemed, employed to rail against, and who, moreover, lacked any kind of perspective when scrutinizing the flaws of lesser mortals. The alternative, I reckoned, was infinitely more attractive. The alternative was to declare myself free.

I don't think I ever 'gave up' religion. I gave up the Catholic Church. I gave up prayer. I gave up 'believing' in God. But I don't think I ever gave up religion, because, inasfar as we understand it now, I don't believe I ever had any to begin with. My father was right about that, except that I wasn't even a decent 'pagan'. My primary feeling towards the Church was anger – unfocused and not particularly rational. And strangely, or perhaps not, it is a small step from being angry with God to deciding He does not exist. I was about to leave my teens and had been flirting with rock 'n' roll and the attendant philosophy of peace and love. This was five years or so before a north Dublin foursome attending Mount Temple School began to make the first tentative steps towards integrating the twin imperatives of God and groove. We had no such vision: the two just didn't go together. Even if you factored out what is now called rock 'n' roll excess, the fact remained that, for all kinds of cultural reasons, God appeared to be incompatible with the path stretching out ahead of us. We had grown up with a model of God centred on authority and control, in which message and meaning had been reduced to a series of 'don'ts'. In the model we had been given, the bottom line appeared to rest on a disavowal of pleasure, at least of the more immediate kinds, and really there appeared not to be much more to the whole religion thing. Pleasure was pretty much coterminous with sin, and brought with it both guilt and fear of punishment. Once it became clear that the enforcers of the doctrine were open to not practising what they preached, the power of the idea of sin began to fragment, and the system that had enforced it began to seem arbitrarily and gratuitously oppressive.

Moreover, there was the fact that disbelief appeared so much, well, smarter. Believing in God was not merely old-fashioned, superstitious and constricting, it was also a sign of weakness, simplicity and fearfulness. We were too clever, too clued in, too cute in every sense you can conceive of, to need crutches. My contemporaries and I were about to set out on an adventure of freedom. We had started to pocket our first pay packets and were determined to let the throttle out. We were going to party, dance, drink, love, and drive fast-looking cars, and we did not want God riding shotgun on such activities.

Looking back now, I cannot recall a single moment of epiphany when I understood, even briefly, the enormity of what I now understand religion to signify. But I have a sense today, acquired several eventful decades later, that I never recall having had as a child, of what religion is, and of what it might offer. The strange thing is that I always had this sense, except that I never thought of it as religion. I had, as a child, an awareness that religion might be important, but no sense of what its content might be. I was aware of the things I now think of religion as containing, but had no idea that these could be called religion.

It was many, many years later that I awoke one morning with a phrase running around my head and, in the background, the sound of a wind swirling through trees, and realized that I had had as a child the most vibrant sense of the religious. The phrase was 'Picture yourself being born . . .' It was all I recalled from a passage I'd read in a book by Fr Luigi Giussani, the Italian priest who founded Communion and Liberation around the time I was, in fact, born. The trees I recognized also, because as I woke I became convinced that I was back in my aunt's house in Cloonyquin, in the County Roscommon countryside, and I was maybe 8 or 9 years old. The book was *The Religious Sense*, in which Giussani, by telling us what religion is, implicitly tells us what religion is not: 'Picture yourself being born, coming out of your mother's womb at the age you are now at this very moment in terms of your development and consciousness. What would be the first, absolutely your initial reaction? If I were to open my eyes for the first time in this instant, emerging from my mother's womb, I would be overpowered by the wonder and awe of things as a "presence". I would be bowled over and amazed by the stupefying repercussion of a presence which is expressed in current language by the word "thing". Things! That's "something"! "Thing", which is a concrete and, if you please, banal version of the word "being". *Being*: not as some abstract entity, but as presence, a presence which I do not myself make, which I find. A presence which imposes itself on me.'

As we grow we forget what it is like to be a child. I don't mean that we necessarily forget what happened or what our thoughts were, but we forget the constant torrent of sensation that childhood is. We become inured to things, indifferent, worn down. We lose our taste for the sharpness of sensation. In that moment of waking, I was returned, not to a childhood memory in the abstract sense, but to a Proustian moment of recall, when the sound of the trees outside my aunt's house was vibrant in my head, as though forty years had been reduced to moments. And with the sound came everything else as well: the scent of the beech, the mystery of O'Rourke's field over the ditch, the wonder of the distance to the main road more than a mile away, the resonance of the phrase – 'the cross' – used to describe the intersection between my aunt's road and the main Roscommon to Boyle road, the very light of some of those many summer days which I and my older sister Marian spent as children in that paradise. In the next minute there unleashed from somewhere inside of me a torrent of such memory: collecting acorns, and particularly their shape and texture, filling bean cans with water from the potholes after rain, the fizz of the lemonade from the picnics we had up beyond French's House, the resonance of names . . . Scramogue, Taluntupeen, the Avenue. From the ages of 4 or 5, we had gone there every summer, sometimes for weeks on end. The year my sister Margaret was born, we spent several months there, from spring through to September.

There was something about Cloonyquin that captivated and excited us beyond anything else. Best known, to the extent that it is known at all, as the birthplace of the songwriter Percy French, it was for us our mother's birthplace, a paradise that contrasted with the drabness of the town of Castlerea (though I remember too the strange attraction the streets of the town had for a couple of days after going home). It was a magical place to be, to lie in bed at night and listen to the quiet of the countryside and the sounds that comprised this quietude. The night there was made of soft and cool, of light airy brushes arising accidentally out of the darkness. Leaf on leaf. Wire on wood. Water on galvanized iron. Together, this host of simultaneous accidents created a web of sound that rolled through to the eardrum like cotton wool, drawing you into its folds. At home in town before sleep, you fought the sounds of the street; here you fell into their embrace and they closed around him.

I remember the 'tunnel of trees' just up from my aunt's house, and there being something ritualistic about running through it on the first evening to where Jimmy, then my aunt's boyfriend, used to live. I only need to pause for a second to tune into a moment shortly after our arrival there when I was 8 or 9 years old: the trees on either side of the road resonating with the racket of the recent rain, droplets tripping from the towering treetops that meet overhead in the centre of the road's airspace, buffeted from leaf to twig to branch as they tumble downwards, slapping and tutting and sighing and moaning as they spit down from their momentary halting places, each drop sounding separately and in unison with the others: on the one hand a plop, a plip, a determined round splat; on the other a hissing, streaming, torrent of sound, like a living machine for distilling and delaying the sensation of rain, which has stopped outside but is captured here in the tunnel for God knows what purpose. All around are sudden cracks and sighs, as if the world might soon awake from a deep sleep. Away in the depths of the trees are plants with shapes and shadows I recognize by sight but never could name: one like a strange, crouching bird that seemed to be alive, another with a sharply featured triangular shaped leaf as green as a front door. In the pockets of light beneath where the tunnel's roof remains unclosed, small clouds of midges have gathered to pass the aeons of time before darkness falls, like pockets of displaced cloud trapped by darkness far from home, terrified and dangerous. We run through the tunnel of weeping leaves with our eyes closed.

Straight ahead on the far side, as the road curves into the climb towards the hayfields and the sun, is the hungry gate of the house where the two Padians lived. The little house stands in its fairytale grandeur silhouetted against the western sky, clearing momentarily before capitulating to the darkness, the sun making a stain of redness that seems to seep through the house like a hand against a light bulb.

In my memory, Miss Padian stands inside the gate, staring deep into the tunnel as though she and she alone is responsible for the hubble-bubble of the weeping trees. In her fingers she holds a lighted cigarette, a wand of white and fire as she stands watching the two little strangers timidly pass on the other side of the road and break into another sudden run. Then the humming of Jimmy's bicycle mingles with the discourse of the tumbling droplets in the tree-tunnel's million leaves, like a stream of running water or something live that couldn't settle, as though the bicycle were a part of this as much as anything, as though it had learned the language of this place and belonged there more than the recently returned and prodigal rain.

Jimmy lifts me onto the bar of the black bike and ushers Marian astride the carrier behind the saddle packed underneath with newspapers. As though our weights make no difference, he pushes the bike forward and begins walking it and its passengers towards the house. As we draw level again with the gate of the Padians' house, he lets go of the right-hand handlebar and lifts his cap to Miss Padian standing at the gate, the cigarette clasped tightly in her lips, her eyes all but closed against the smoke. She mouths a greeting without removing the cigarette from her lips. She seems not to know it is there. As we pause for the adults to exchange their rudimentary phrases about the weather, I watch the ash waggle slightly, waiting for the moment when it falls off, but instead it grows and grows until there is more ash than cigarette, then hardly anything but ash at all.

Those weeks we spent at our Aunt Teresa's were the most intense of our childhoods, and, when the holidays were over, we had to be dragged screaming into my father's van to be brought back to Castlerea. Now, forty years later, I was awaking to the reality that, as a child, I had, like all children, the most intense experience of religion. I had encountered reality and been overcome by it, by the wonder of it and the intensity of it. I had, on a moment-to-moment basis, been experiencing a profound sense of the religious reality, but nobody had ever told me that this is what it was.

It reminds me a little of the first time I ever saw a television set. It was sometime in the early 1960s. I had never heard the word 'television', still less had the faintest idea what it might be. But one day I observed that a crowd had gathered around the window of Sonny Coyne's radio shop just up the street, staring in at something. I joined the edge of the crowd and craned my neck to see. I could make out nothing between the coats of the adults, but, after a while, settled on a moderately colourful poster on the window. This, I supposed, was what they were looking at. I stared at it for a while, determined to experience whatever it was that was attracting the adults, but after a while I grew bored. Still, strangely, I stayed, staring at the poster. And still the crowd grew, and by now I was in the middle of a much larger gathering. I thought, 'Well. It's a really nice poster, but have these people not got something better to do?' I was about to leave when the crowd shifted slightly, enabling me to see, over at the corner of the shop, something moving. On a grey, flaky screen, there was a, yes, a moving ship, looming large through what looked like snow. I was astonished and for the first time understood why all the people were there. The strange thing is that, under the influence of the crowd, I had been prepared to stay for the poster, which I had become so convinced held some intense significance. My sense of my childhood experience of religion is a little like that: nobody ever told me, and it never dawned on me, that religion was anything to do with the taste of reality and the awe I felt at being alive in a world filled with wonder.

# — 2 —

# Pan's People

The sound from the guitar strapped around my neck with an improvised belt seemed to change utterly a landscape I'd been looking at
for eighteen years. The sound was brittle, yet solid, dirty and loud,
distorted and angry. It uttered forth at the merest touch of the
fingers. I adjusted my grip on the red plectrum and began to address
the strings with a determined downward stroke. The character of the
sound was immediately changed. It became more assertive, fuller,
more insistent, grinding like a chainsaw striving to cut through a
wooden boxful of bottles, or a jackhammer tearing spitefully at
concrete. I began to play in an indeterminate sequence the three
chords I'd learned – D, G and A – becoming lost in the noise I was
making, allowing my gaze to pan across the full extent of the view
from the skylight of the attic of our house looking out over the River
Suck. I observed the dull yellow of the late-winter grass, the tapering
river, slightly swollen from three weeks of relentless rain, the spindly
skeletons of trees, and how all of it suddenly appeared to have a new
shape and meaning. Everything seemed more assertive, more determined, overwhelming the normal sense of monotony and dullness.
It was as though I was seeing the landscape through someone else's
eyes. The river cut through the countryside with a new panache,
leaving the bank behind it sharper, more defined. The tree I had
climbed in boyhood now pointed skywards in a defiant claw. Even
when I stopped sawing at the strings, the effect remained for a
minute or more. I stood there listening to the familiar sounds
drifting across the rooftops from the street: the traffic, the shouts,
the high-heeled shoes, the tumbling of beer kegs, a pneumatic drill
somewhere in the middle distance. For a brief moment some kind of
reconciliation was effected between the sounds and the view I'd

witnessed as a single reality throughout childhood but had never thought of as connected. I walked across the attic floor as though across a stage, through the tea-chests and cardboard boxes full of books, papers and cast-off clothes from America, as though they were amplifiers, monitors, crazy boxes. I knelt down at the source of the sound I had just made, an old Pye wireless belonging to my father. The sound had ceased and nothing of it remained, and yet it seemed that everything had altered beyond recognition. Although the guitar in my hands was a cheap cast-off that had already been flayed to within an inch of its flimsy life by my best friend Gerry, I felt closer to it than to any object I had ever possessed. I liked the deep, dark redness of it, the hollowness of its cutaway body, the feel of its strings. My fingers moved stiffly to shape again the difficult D chord that Gerry had shown me. I adjusted the black microphone clipped to the body of the guitar and attached to a wonky cassette player, which in turn was wired into the old Pye wireless set. The astonishing sound that resulted had emerged from the accidental discovery that, by linking in the speaker of the old wireless to the headphone socket and depressing simultaneously the record, play and pause buttons, the machine functioned as a makeshift amplifier. I moved my recalcitrant fingers clumsily into the G shape. A discordant sound, between a whistle and a screech, pierced the cold air of the attic. It sounded like the opening of *Pretty Vacant*, the astonishing Sex Pistols' record I'd heard on the *John Peel Show*. The piercing sound built into a frenzied scream of feedback.

At this point I had never even kissed a girl, but I had been to bed with John Peel about 400 times. Every night I took the transistor radio to bed with me, and listened to Peel through an earpiece under the blankets. Our affair started in 1972 and lasted nearly a decade. His programme, *Top Gear*, went out on BBC Radio One at 10 p.m. weekdays except Monday, which belonged to Whispering Bob Harris, who, because he actually spoke in a whisper, which fared badly from the high level of static interference on the AM band, could be heard only as an occasional throaty bass note on the wind from Blighty. Peel's confident, paragraphed delivery carried better. The reception in Roscommon was erratic, at the mercy of daylight and weather. I would take the back off the transistor and with a tiny screwdriver adjust the capacitors and resistors when Beefheart grew faint or Eno made sense. Afterwards, I avoided listening to Tangerine Dream, knowing they wouldn't be half as good without the static.

Or perhaps it was something else that caused me to avoid listening. This thought struck me when I read Paul Morley's brilliant 2003 book, *Words and Music: A History of Pop in the Shape of a City*. He was talking about Kraftwerk, another band I remember from those Blanket Street nights. 'Kraftwerk', he wrote, 'were sad. Sad about some things. Sad about other things. It was the sadness of life, the sadness that life goes, in ways that are beyond reason, very much more nowhere than somewhere. It was the sadness of knowing that you must try hard to head somewhere knowing that really we are nowhere. The sadness of doing something knowing it all comes to nothing. The sadness that the excitement of experience dissolves into an eternity beyond experience.' When I heard Kraftwerk I didn't think of them as sad. But I felt sad, just as, hearing other bands, I felt different things. The grown-up world tended then, as it does now, to regard youthful obsession with music as simply an expression of some yearning for identity – a noise with which to declare oneself. It isn't that hardly at all, but mainly a search for meaning, for affirmation, comfort and self-recognition. It is an intellectual, an imaginative and a spiritual search, and it is directed at pop culture because the known, conventional world fails to echo the young person's sense of wonder and attraction.

The Ireland of the early years of *Top Gear* would be completely unrecognizable to today's Ireland, saturated in pop culture and youth obsession. Then, pop music was all but illegal, meriting a couple of hours weekly on national radio. The national radio station, RTE, had one hour of rock 'n' roll – *Ken's Club* on Friday evening – and if you didn't like Steely Dan you were in the wrong shop. Nobody at an official level seemed to think this situation in the least bit inappropriate or odd. In the UK, John Peel cleared a space for rock 'n' roll to breathe, making an immense contribution to the extension of its social and political reach. But in Ireland, where there was no youth culture, his influence probably went much further. Arguably, it was largely down to the impact of *Top Gear* that Irish music radio developed as it did in the 1970s, beginning with the pirate boom and culminating in RTE Radio 2, which ushered in a pop revolution when it opened in 1979. The burgeoning rock scene of 1970s' Dublin might never have developed had not John Peel been there feeding the dreams and imaginations of a generation of young musicians. And though I never heard him enthuse much about the music of either band, it is not implausible to suggest that, had Peel not existed, neither would the Boomtown Rats or U2, Ireland's most famous contributions to international pop culture.

Peel was less a DJ than a teacher, although he rarely got into historiography or analysis. He just presented and enthused about the music he played at such a level of wit and intelligence as to convey a sense of the music's significance and connectedness without breaking the spell of wonder and magic. He was described following his death as an 'eternal teenager', but this is an outsider's condescension. Peel was ever young but always old too, like an owl. When I first saw his photograph I thought him venerable, but he never seemed to grow older. He was fatherly in a new way, and spiritual in an old way, though the content of that spirituality seemed incongruous and implausible.

To listen to Peel through the fog of static from the isolation of teenage fear and boredom, to hear him introduce with a note of irony or whimsy something from the latest record by Lou Reed or The Only Ones was to be uplifted in oneself, to be transported to a different level of reality, to find hope, to know faith and to experience meaning. I don't, for the moment, claim this as a spiritual experience, but I do insist that the phenomenon, as I experienced it, filled the parts of my imagination that religion should properly have filled but had failed to.

We in Ireland continue to have a strange view of Irish culture, which, for all it disparages what is purely Irish, appears ignorant too of other things that moulded what we are. The problem is not simply the fiction of Irishness created by colonization and the way we reacted to it, but has to do with perceiving correctly the true effects of influences that ran counter to the approved, official culture, constructed post-independence as evidence of our recovery from foreign occupation. Even yet, nearly a century later, we divide the world into Irish and non-Irish, and perceive the 'alien' influence as a largely irrelevant accident, good or bad depending on where we stand. With British cultural influences, we seem conscious only of having experienced them in some accidental, spillover sense, without really being affected. Though many of these phenomena nurtured us when we had little to breathe with, we consider them much as they are considered in their own place, attributing importance according to scale rather than significance. It is as though the true history of our living culture has not yet been drafted, never mind understood, as though the complex truth must remain a secret history understood only by a minority who imagine themselves misfits. Self-understanding is lost between the twin concepts of what we were told we should become and what we sought to become out of a petulance born of starvation. That the reality is neither, but inextricably both, is something no element of our public apparatus seems capable of articulating.

A similar process seems to have afflicted our religious life. Irish Catholicism was a product of dire necessity and the post-colonial imagination. It defined itself more by what it was not, than by what it might be. It was not Protestant. It was not pagan. It was not of England. The trouble was that, since Anglicanism was, in all the most fundamental respects, indistinguishable from Catholicism, the emphasis of Irish Catholicism tended to be placed on the peripherals. Discussion of Catholicism in Ireland tends generally to focus on issues of politics, morality, identity, culture and power, with almost no allusion to the core content of Christianity, or even very much mention of Christianity's central figure, Jesus Christ. While writing this book, I sat, as a member of the Broadcasting Commission of Ireland, at a hearing held for the purpose of selecting from two applicants for a Christian broadcasting licence. There was much talk of 'the Christian community', 'family values' and 'uplifting' music, but the name of Jesus was never once mentioned. Whole books are written about Irish Catholicism in which Jesus is referred to rarely, if at all. Mention of Catholicism in Ireland nowadays is usually taken as a reference to the 'moral' programme associated with Catholicism, relating to sex and procreation. There is a historical context for this, which I outlined in some detail in my 1997 book, *An Intelligent*

*Person's Guide to Modern Ireland*. When the primitive nature of pre-Famine Irish Christianity – reputedly joyful, playful, magical, sensual – was suppressed by the Church, it was partly by way of defining Irishness against the alleged decadence and immorality of the colonizer and the prior licentiousness that had supposedly led the people into disaster. Thus, my father's references to 'pagans' was simply another way of asserting the moral superiority of Catholicism. It was through control of the family and the sexual life of the people that the Church developed a virtual monopoly of Irish morality, which allowed it to exercise both civil and physical control, so becoming obsessed with the exercise of social power rather than with the spiritual nourishment of the people. This, in turn, was to be the source of its undoing.

I remember the moment when I started to become an agnostic. I didn't 'decide' this, so much as make a decision which had this outcome as its inevitable consequence. It was a Saturday evening in the summer of 1974. I had just turned 19 and was home for the weekend from my new job as a railway clerk in a town more than twenty miles away, which at the time seemed a great distance. Although I had been breathing in the new culture of the time for several years, I had not as yet seen the necessity to make a choice between this and the lazy Catholicism that I'd been growing up with. I left home that evening with the intention of going to confession. I vaguely recall that this was part of some special project of petitioning I had started with a view to seeking God's assistance in getting off with a particular girl I fancied. Thus far, my entreaties had seemed to fall on deaf ears, and I was unable to shake off the suspicion that this was because my soul was besmirched by various darkish, if not especially significant, stains. I had decided that a clean sheet might put me in a better situation to receive the Creator's blessing for my desires. On the way to the church, however, I fell into bad company – several older guys I used to play soccer with on the fair green and elsewhere, who were going to play pool in a local pub. They persuaded me to join them and then prevailed upon me to partake of a glass of cider. During the pool game, I listened to their talk about girls. They were funny and outrageous and made the whole thing sound much less solemn than I had begun to imagine. I became convinced that I needed to invest less energy in prayer and a little extra effort in becoming more like these guys. Not only did I not go to confession, but the entire experience seemed to offer me a wholly new approach to dealing with life. I could take control of my life and make things happen with it. I was not a prisoner of reality: I was free.

By an odd happenstance, the story of my own burst for freedom, because it resonates in certain ways with that of the society in which I made it, has frequently allowed me to grasp things that were happening around me to the extent that such phenomena were reflections of things that had happened in my own life. In some ways, it seems to me, Irish society's searching has tended to parallel my own.

Unlike other European societies, Ireland never had a clear moment of youth rebellion, at which the authority of the old was questioned or jettisoned, but we did have a more extended and subtle process in which the same thing occurred on a piecemeal basis. When I was young, youth was to be seen and not heard. As I grew older, youth became more and more vocal and important. God, because He was old and authoritarian, became a casualty of this shift, though by no means the only one.

I think societies, like individuals, have an unconscious sense of their own age. I don't mean chronological age calculated since some point of clear historical beginning, like independence, but rather age in terms of attitude, ambition, outlook and self-understanding, the way a society thinks and speaks of itself. Put another way, every society has, as the dominant chord of its culture, a deep-down sense of being either young, pre-pubescent, middle-aged or old. This tendency may once have been a subtle presence, but now, as a result of the influence of mass media, it is an inescapable feature of modern societies. If a society is, in some respects, like an individual, a media-dominated society is much more so. A media-saturated society thinks of its life as something requiring movement and achievement within a certain imaginable and manageable period of time. It perceives its life progressing in a linear fashion, and measures this progress against, perhaps, past failures, past stagnation, past repression. The average educated citizen of a Western economy tends to perceive his or her adult life as something to be realized over roughly three decades. By 50, most people feel they have arrived wherever it is they thought they were going, or they have developed a sense that their life has become directionless and lost. Either way, they will view that life within the ambit of a certain journey, and perceive themselves, at any given moment, to be at a certain point of achievement or non-achievement on that journey. Along the trajectory of an average life, from the age of about 20 to about 50, there is a constant measuring of progress according to a perhaps inchoate and unstated plan, a set of aspirations, a fantasy, a dream. This is how we measure success or failure in ourselves. And so it is with societies that have become hyper-conscious of their own collective aspirations: they think, as it were, like human beings. Sometimes this process is defined in the journey towards self-realization from a moment of revolution – a tribal project driven not by talk but by action; in others, it is measured by prosperity in the wake of a recession, or some other calamity. In Ireland, as with so many of the phenomena associated with the shift from tradition to modernity, this cultural shift seemed to occur faster and more intensely than elsewhere. Ireland is not unique, but it may, in this sense, offer the possibility of observing many of the phenomena associated with modernity in a laboratory setting, having a combination of post-revolutionary consciousness and sudden hyper-media awareness feeding into the same sense of self. Seeing things literally, then, you might decide that Irish society is now, in the early years of a new millennium, in its mid-80s, having been born in 1921. But in truth, that post-revolutionary consciousness is now all but dissipated, and there emerges a much more important moment, in terms of the way we regard reality: the introduction of television and the explosion of the media and counter-cultural phenomena that occurred in the 1960s. This began a process of self-scrutiny that has caused us to reimagine ourselves as a modernizing society and to make this the dominant element of our collective thought.

The opening up to new ideas and possibilities facilitated by television, and the focusing of public discussion on the box in the corner – for many years on a single channel – caused a heightened sense of particularity to develop in what might be called the public consciousness of Irish society. From this there emerged a new 'we', to

supplant the 'we' defined by the calamitous events of late nineteenth-
and early twentieth-century Irish history, which defined the national
story in the minds of my father's generation. When, in the 1970s,
1980s and 1990s, we talked about 'us', we knew instantly what we
meant: a new generation that had taken over moral ownership of
Ireland from those who had failed her. There were arguments about
details, but also a sense that differences about these did not amount
to much of a problem. There was diversity of opinion, perspective
and experience, to a degree, but not enough to dilute the emerging
sense of a society growing in a relatively single-minded way. Ireland
wasn't, for example, like Britain, where there was, as well as a devel-
oping multiracial society, a strong sense of class division. In Ireland,
as we nudged ourselves forward into a mass-media society, in which
the collective condition would become subject to intense and
constant scrutiny, there was always a sense of a search for a single
strain of thinking that would define us all. And Irish society was, at
this point of reinvention, increasingly young. The centres of power,
it is true, were operated mainly by old men, but the emerging energy
of the society was very much a youthful one, and this, combined with
the increasingly particularized nature of the incoming cultural influences, created the ideal conditions for a kind of revolution. In a
sense, it was tacitly decided that the first revolution, the one that
unfurled from 1916, and indeed the devotional revolution that
preceded it, had failed, or had gone off the rails. And now, here, was
another opportunity. So, roughly a half-century later, although there
was no declaration or even initiatory acknowledgement, we started
over.

Half-jokingly, I would hazard the suggestion that, in terms of the
imagination it developed at the point of this renewal of consciousness, Irish society is now hitting 50. I make this calculation as
follows: it is generally agreed that the sixties didn't arrive in Ireland
until 1970, so if we decide, reasonably enough, that Irish society
entered its teens in 1970, its 20s in 1977, its 30s in 1987, and its 40s
in 1997, we arrive now at the half-century of Ireland's undeclared
modern era. Oddly, or perhaps not, this would make the society, in
terms of its imagination, roughly the same chronological age as
myself. These are approximate dates, to be sure, but I am doubly

attracted to them because, strangely, each of the years in question marks a critical general election, events which, however imperfectly, seem to be connected to the staged shifting in the development of Irish political life.

While attempts to discover patterns in Irish life by means of a generational analysis will inevitably throw up a host of inconsistencies and contradictions, there is nevertheless a remarkable degree of clarity to be divined in such broad strokes. The era of seismic change that has occurred in Ireland in the past half-century was ushered in by the generation now in its late 50s and 60s. The 1960s' generation seized power by unseating the 'traditionalist' incumbents, and maintained its hold by perpetuating a war against largely phantom notions of conservatism and reaction. This generation has held on to power until now, though it is currently beginning to wane. The 1970s' generation, to which I belonged, was largely sidelined, or at most achieved bit-part participation in society. The 1980s' generation became perhaps largely irrelevant, because it left, virtually en masse, when emigration started up again following a short reprieve known as the Lemass Spring. The 1990s' generation, although it stayed, became perhaps even more detached from society than any of its predecessors. These young people opted, and were enabled, to stay in Ireland, but by and large did not wish to get involved, other than to the extent of participating in the economy. The generation emerging now, in the first decade of the third millennium, may take everyone by surprise. It remains inscrutable. It does not appear to think in the way that young people are imagined to think.

The undeniable frivolity of the 1990s was an attempt to conceal the relative marginalization of young people from politics and society, a kind of ironic sour grapes to hide the sense of hurt generated by the failure of the generation in power to hand on any sense of citizenship or patriotism, or indeed anything that might be regarded as a sense of inherited communality. Young people have been carefully cultivated to take a minimal interest in politics or social affairs, and as a result the passions of the younger generations appear to focus mainly on work and leisure and, to the extent that there is a cultural manifestation of their aspirations, on the pursuit of some ethic of engagement to enable them to be part of Irish society without committing to it. Younger people have, mostly and broadly, accepted the model of society with which they have been presented. But they have also encountered a blockage of the imagination in relation to what might happen next. They do not want to go back, but cannot see any inviting space into which to move forward. The notion that there is some 'postmodern' way of re-ringing the changes is one that attracts them, but nobody has the faintest idea, other than via a retreat into 'irony', what this might actually mean.

The confusion of today's young people is the inevitable consequence of their being conned by the rhetoric of the present generation in power, which has convinced them, because it has convinced itself, that the journey started in the 1960s is, whatever its momentary imperfections, the One True Journey, the only possible route towards enlightenment and contentment, the only possible way to reach the End of History. Nobody uses these terminologies, of course, but they are implicit in virtually every contribution to public debate from what is deemed to be a 'progressive' quarter.

When you consider many of the key events in Irish life and politics in the past four decades, it becomes clear that Ireland is now a nation in middle age, but with a particular complexion, which might be diagnosed as a reluctance to grow any older. I call this condition 'Peter Pan Syndrome', a phrase which, having fancied I coined it, I came across retrospectively in articles grappling with similar ideas in a number of British newspaper articles. The roots of this culture are interesting and instructive as to the underlying conditions. The culture, because it is a shallow and largely neurotic reaction to an earlier reality, is not what it appears. It is not, for example, the confident modernity it claims to be.

Let us begin with the end of the old world, the world embodied by my father, but by the mid-1970s corrupted by pseudo-respectability and a lack of imagination. In Ireland, as elsewhere, the main challenge to what remained of the previous establishment came in the late 1960s and 1970s, feeding in from the outside world, from a generation in other Western societies inspired by the pop culture of the sixties and the student rebel rhetoric of 1968 and beyond. This generation did not properly take hold in Ireland until the ascent to power of the second coalition government of Garret FitzGerald in 1983, but even by the late 1970s, power was already being transferred from those who had assumed it pretty much continuously since the foundation of the State. Largely, it was transferred to a generation suffering from a profound anger, and possibly, in clinical terms, a deep neurosis, arising from perceptions of the abuses of power that had occurred throughout its youth, and from a sense of disappointment with the failure to deliver on the promises of the 1916 Proclamation and, indeed, the essential content of Christianity. For this generation, Catholicism had nothing to offer except accusation, proscription and oppression. The anger was undoubtedly justified, and it was certainly real. There was a sense that Ireland, through a misplaced obsession with restoring a dead culture, had lost pace with the world, and an even stronger sense that the Catholic Church had ceased to be a conduit for Christian or spiritual values, and was reduced to a power base, obsessed with control. Briefly, for a handful of years around where the 1960s met the 1970s, there had been an upsurge of optimism, based on the Lemass economic spring, but this had dissipated by the mid-1970s, leaving the national pool of hope as stagnant as before. The problem expressed itself in two words: old men.

By the mid-1970s, although the demographics of the country had altered radically to make the under-25s into a majority for the first time since the Famine, the culture of society was as grey and grizzled as it is possible to imagine. But young people were wising up, acquiring their own cultural weaponry, and were moreover driven by an intense anger towards the era just passing, in which they had been at best ignored and, more usually, subjected to violence and contempt.

The government in power at that time was the 1973–77 Fine Gael/Labour coalition, led by Liam Cosgrave, which seemed to embody in its very demeanour the national mood which was characterized by entropy and ennui. Defined by its hair-shirt economic policies and dead-handed social conservatism, this administration was vaguely defined as 'Christian Democratic', but really suggests itself in hindsight as perhaps the closest we have come to replicating the moribund communist regimes of Eastern Europe. Cosgrave was a kind of sub-Brezhnev figure, surrounded by a politburo of grey-suited reactionaries who, perhaps more than any Irish government before or since, mobilized the ire and impatience of the young. At the heart of the tedium was a spark of hope, and his name was Garret FitzGerald. He was tall and articulate and had a fuzzy head, which at the time we thought to be purely a hairdressing phenomenon. He didn't speak in the kind of gnawing, wheedling accent normally associated with politicians, but in a crisp, internationalist burr, with a tendency towards long words and complicated sentences. He was handsome in a kind of academic way, and had an air about him that was to be retrospectively recognized as European. He was the kind of politician who could be 'let out' abroad. Above all, he was, comparatively speaking, young. (In 1977, when he became leader of Fine Gael, he was 51. That, then, was young.) He was the kind of leader who, when he came on TV, had a tendency to annoy my father, and, for precisely that reason, a capacity to inspire arguments between us. 'See?' you might say, to a roomful of adults. 'See what I mean? At last someone who knows what he's talking about.'

In retrospect, it has more or less been decided that FitzGerald was a disappointment, maybe even a bit of a fraud. But this is perhaps the conclusion that is reached about every politician who does not die suddenly at the hands of an assassin. It is important to stress, odd as it may seem nowadays, that FitzGerald in his heyday had the capacity to energize and electrify young Irish people as no one had done before and no one has since. Within Cosgrave's Fine Gael, FitzGerald had been a minor thorn in the side of the leadership, taking a libertarian view on 'social' issues such as contraception, on which the Church had dominated the agenda until then, and an unfashionably ethical one on issues such as police brutality, then an emerging scandal, partly owing to the overflow of paramilitarism from across the border.

FitzGerald's primary refrain was to do with creating in the Republic a pluralist, non-sectarian state, which might become more palatable for Unionists in the North. The first *Magill Book of Politics* (1981) said of FitzGerald: '[His] political rhetoric is often quite radical but the solutions he postulates, if any, are invariably very conservative.' But in government in the 1980s, surrounded by people such as Alan Dukes, Nuala Fennell, Monica Barnes, Alan Shatter and John Kelly, and with the support of Labour aspirants such as Dick Spring and Ruairi Quinn, he cut quite a dash through the cob-webbed undergrowth of Irish public affairs. In truth, as it turned out, FitzGerald was indeed every bit as conservative as those against whom he railed. Or at least, the circumstances in which he found himself caused his radicalism to be reduced to a husk of itself. This was perhaps inevitable. For one thing, the party he came to lead had long been the refuge of some of the most reactionary forces in Irish society. And, even though he greatly expanded Fine Gael's numeri-cal strength, he did so by simply adding a kind of progressive extension to an essentially moribund entity. Whereas his rhetoric was unfailingly radical, his actions seemed always to be predicated on the need to coax young people up on the front of his trailer without losing the hardcore party faithful off the back. Hence, he embarked upon perhaps the most successful confidence trick ever perpetrated in Irish politics. FitzGerald brought to Irish politics a pandering to the iconography of youth that had earlier delivered for Harold Wilson in the UK. He posed for photographers with Bono in Windmill Lane and informed reporters that his favourite pop song was the Byrds' 'Turn! Turn! Turn!' (This song, whose words are taken from the Book of Ecclesiastes, is arguably the oldest pop lyric in existence!) This started a trend.

In 1984, in advance of that year's Bob Dylan concert at Slane, the chronologically youthful leader of the Labour Party, Dick Spring, was pictured on the cover of the capital's listing magazine, *In Dublin*, with a copy of Bob Dylan's *Bringing It All Back Home*, and inside wrote, no doubt sincerely, of his personal favourites from the Dylan back-catalogue: '"Blowin' in the Wind" and "The Times They Are A-changin"', he said, 'are clichés only if "We Shall Overcome" is a cliché. And it isn't. What Dylan was writing about then – prejudice and bigotry in the United States – is still a potent force all over the world. In countries that cannot tolerate ideas, in societies that cling to the superiority of one sex over the other, in places where race and colour are grounds for discrimination, the answer is still blowin' in the wind. And that wind, all over the world, is gathering strength.' In this paragraph, Dick Spring was effectively setting out the mani-festo of the Peter Pan Generation. Though himself unconvincing in the part, he was using the universal language of the rock 'n' roll culture to define how he and his generation of politicians would tap into the increasingly youthful imagination of the Irish electorate, and meet its appetite for change.

It has to be clearly understood that FitzGerald and Spring were speaking to a completely depoliticized generation, for whom civil war politics had not been supplanted by anything remotely ideological, and for whom there had as yet been no tangible focus for its youthful energies. And yet this was also a generation fired by enormous angers of a social nature. The overwhelming consciousness of the time was that Ireland had been badly served by those in whose stewardship it had rested since independence, that these worthies had, in effect, held back the progress of Ireland in the world. In time, this came to be measured by various ever-present yardsticks: the extent to which Catholic Ireland had fallen out of step with the modern world; the sense of how inhospitable nationalist Ireland was to Unionism; and the extent to which unfavourable comparisons with the new possibilities glimpsed nightly on television provided a measure of Irish backwardness in developmental, cultural and libertarian matters. The vaguely liberal, politically correct sentiments expressed by, among others, FitzGerald and Spring, were, in this context, calculated to be far more effective in wooing the youth vote than the turgidly worded panaceas of Karl Marx or James Connolly. Spring stood for what he outlined in his Bob Dylan tribute: the vague sense of a revolution of good guys over bad, of nice-sounding notions of justice and equality and truth. It wasn't so much that he didn't believe in these ideas, or that they weren't, up to a point, real, but there is in retrospect an unmistakable sense that what he really believed in was the idea of him and us believing in them: him being seen to believe in them, and seeming radical for that alone, and us beginning to reimagine ourselves in that way. We were beginning to fall in love not so much with the ideals themselves as with the idea of idealism, especially when set in opposition to stagnation and decay.

Something significant happened in journalism around this time also, and this was to become especially crucial in my own life. The period of the late 1970s was undoubtedly unique in the stretch of time since the foundation of the State, in that Irish society spat forth a generation of commentators comprising not career journalists, but idealistic young people who sought to take ownership of society and kick it into a different shape. At the time, there emerged a raft of alternative media, including current affairs magazines such as *Magill*, 'entertainment' magazines such as *In Dublin* and *Hot Press*, and dozens of pirate radio stations of varying quality and intent. The overwhelming sentiment of these, in that indisputably repressive environment, was softly leftist. That there was never any real ideological depth to this is perhaps why it latched on to the hope offered by FitzGerald and for a time followed his wagon in the belief that his 'Constitutional Crusade', and the implementation of the 'liberal agenda' (contraception, divorce and abortion) was the way to make a mark on Irish society and sweep away the establishment. To a large extent, the 'establishment' meant the Catholic Church. FitzGerald cunningly manipulated these energies, succeeding in having himself accepted as the radical, wholesome alternative to an allegedly deeply conservative Fianna Fáil. FitzGerald's 'Constitutional Crusade', building on the foundations of Declan Costello's 'Just Society' prescription, spearheaded the massive social upheavals of the 1980s and 1990s and brought about the defeat of what used to be called 'the forces of tradition'. Although FitzGerald himself had retired from politics by the time the fruits of his influence became manifest, there is no gainsaying the assessment that the targets he identified in his crusade were achieved, at least on the terms understood at the time. Divorce and contraception have been facts of Irish life for some years now, and it seems as if it is only a matter of time before the abortion debate is resolved in much the same manner as in other Western societies. Moreover, the debates about these issues have fundamentally altered the nature of Irish life, eroding the power of the previous monoliths and promoting a new sense of personal freedom among individual citizens.

This evolving reality was to change my life most profoundly and immediately. In the late 1970s I started to submit articles on spec to the rock 'n' roll magazine *Hot Press*. Some were published, some not, but eventually, in 1984, I was offered a full-time job on the magazine. Suddenly I found myself at the very centre of the Peter Pan revolution.

The technique of the Peter Pan generation in power, which is to pretend that it never won power at all but is still fighting a rearguard action against the forces of darkness from the past, has provided the main engine of public life in Ireland for two decades. Thus, the Catholic Church, de Valera's Ireland, the GAA, Fianna Fáil and any form of nationalistic expression became the straw men whose toppling before the advance of the Peter Pans would mark the onward march of the revolution. The dominant idea of Irish life and what should be its natural trajectory, conveyed on any given day by the mainstream media, is that a marginalized bunch of radical voices, left-leaning and liberal, is still seeking to overthrow an establishment dominated by Catholic thinking, nationalist politics, traditional conservatism, cute hoorism and patriarchal supremacism. Of course, there are in reality hardly any Catholics, nationalists, traditionalists, conservatives, cute hoors or patriarchs left, but this is a minor inconvenience which does not in any way dilute the determination of this plucky band of radicals to free itself from tyranny and oppression. The Peter Pan ideology is protected by its own self-evident morality and by the promulgation of the idea that it and its adherents remain under grave threat. Such is its correctness about everything that no dissent is possible other than that promoted by itself, and anything not falling into this category is *ipso facto* part of an 'establishment' backlash, a counter-revolution designed to frustrate its plucky assault on the citadels of power.

I have, for much of the past two decades, found myself belonging to this culture and yet being troubled by it. Instinctively, I find all its ideas appealing; I want to belong to it. The people of the post-1960s' revolution have always seemed to me the most interesting, the most entertaining, the most creative and the most fun-loving. Confronted with a choice between accepting their entire worldview and inviting a return of the greyness that preceded them, you would need to be insane not to embrace them wholeheartedly. And yet I have been troubled, too, by the inconsistencies of their prescriptions, with their blindness towards the flaws in their beliefs, and the strengths in some of the values they have devoted themselves to sweeping away. The problem with them is not so much with the values they preach as with their absolute unwillingness to admit that the world did not begin in 1968, that, along with the greyness and drabness that preceded our revolution, there were things in the world that might be worth preserving.

A few years after I wrote *An Intelligent Person's Guide to Modern Ireland*, I read in an academic tome of some considerable turgidity a reference to one chapter of that book entitled 'On How God Has been Kidnapped and Held to Ransom'. The chapter was an attempt to analyse the reasons for the failure of the Catholic Church in Ireland to capture the imagination of the people with arguably the most sensational story every told. My analysis at that point did not extend much beyond the social context of Catholicism, but within that context I was, if I may say so, scathingly critical of the Irish Church. I criticized the manner in which the Church had appropriated God in Irish society and then, in effect, threatened to withhold Him unless it got its own way. I outlined what I described as parallel forms of colonization, from London and Rome, and described the calamitous effects of these phenomena. I criticized, too, the culture of violence that had attended the Catholic-run Irish system of education, and lamented the joyless version of religiosity we had inherited from history. I also wrote about my attempts to discover for myself some alternative strand of spiritual adventure, using as an example a period some years earlier when I had fallen into the habit of attending a Latin-rite mass in a Dublin city-centre church. 'Coming up to the end of the 1980s,' I wrote, 'although I had not been a regular church-goer for more than a decade, I got into the habit of attending the Tridentine Rite Mass at St Michael and John's Church on Dublin's Quays. I did not have what might be called a "reason" for going. I had long since thought myself out of the Catholic Church, at least in the sense of belonging to its institutional manifestation. But in Ireland, although there are Catholics, lapsed Catholics, non-Catholics and anti-Catholics, there is no such thing as an ex-Catholic. Despite my intellectual antipathy to the institutional church, the lure of the Latin Mass, remembered from boyhood, was enough to get me out of bed on a Sunday morning.' A few years later, someone sent me a newly published academic work with a note alerting me to the fact that one of the chapters briefly touched on this book of mine. A glance at the index led me to the following paragraph: 'To John Waters, who admits to attending the services of the Tridentine Church, "[t]here is no such thing as an ex-Catholic in Ireland."' The scholar went on: 'A more balanced view might be that the disaffection of the traditional church has led many to a spiritual quest of their own.'

This brief extract tells us much about the present culture of Irish society and how it bears down on us in subtle and not so subtle ways. Note that I had not simply 'written' or 'recalled' that I had attended a Tridentine Rite mass – I had 'admitted' it and was, as a consequence, unbalanced.

In writing this chapter of my book, I had had no idea that I was 'admitting' to attending the services of a Tridentine Church. In fact, I stated that I had attended such services for a time and sought to explore my own reasons for doing so. And my reasons for doing so, like – as I speculated – the reasons of others who attended, had to do, precisely, with, yes, a spiritual quest of my own. My reference to ex-Catholics was, of course, both ironic and semantic, a play on phraseology but with a deeper point concerning the impossibility of ever shaking off a Catholic upbringing. The academic, in her simplicity or malice, sought to cite my phrase as a literalism, thus suggesting that I was some kind of defender of reactionary religious traditions. My intention was so obvious that I was at first prompted to wonder why she had bothered to lift the quotation at all (since it made the same point she was seeking to make), and then why, if she was intent on quoting something of mine, she felt obliged to misrepresent it. Of course, I was being naive. She quoted it precisely so she could mangle it, to set me up as a straw man in her thesis. After all, what is the point in railing against nostalgic reactionaries if you cannot find any of the breed in existence?

This is a snapshot of the public culture of Ireland now. The influence of the Peter Pan generation – the way it has assumed office and uses power, the disingenuous way it presents itself, the way it stifles debate and demonizes its critics, the way it hogs both the centres of power and the platforms of protest – has caused, and continues to cause, a cultural dislocation in the evolution of Irish society. It refuses to take responsibility for its own beliefs and their consequences when put into practice. It confuses the young by usurping their natural right to protest. It is turning the mass of citizens away from any kind of interaction with public life, and obscuring the true nature of oppression in modern society. It stands in the doorway and blocks up the hall, preventing discussion of some of the most fundamental aspects of life in Ireland now. Youth, once wasted on the young, is now squandered on the middle-aged. Because of the singular obsessiveness of the Peter Pan generation, the iconography of personal freedom has become so enshrined in the psyche of present-day Ireland that it is not possible to argue as to its limits without setting off an extreme reaction based on either a real or invented fear that that freedom will be snatched away. An everyday practical example of the syndrome's downside, providing an emblem of the overall failure, is that, although the great liberal Holy Grail of divorce has been secured, the fall-out from marital breakdown is brutalizing a significant minority in society beyond what might remotely be deemed inevitable, but nobody will tackle the issue because this could be read as acknowledging that conservatives might have had a few good arguments about the downside of divorce. Because the battle was so hard and so recently won, there is a sense that its consequences cannot be questioned without yielding to the 'forces of reaction' believed to be out there still in the undergrowth.

And so, while family and social life tend towards collapse, and the actually existing youth of our societies are caught in the grip of crime, addiction and apathy, the pseudo-young establishment preaches the further implementation of its palpably inadequate agenda as a solution to the growing senselessness, for which it refuses to acknowledge any form of responsibility. From the culture of a generation ago, which ignored its young, we have moved into one that lionizes everything to do with youth. Countless radio stations play pop and rock around the clock, and the coverage of rock 'n' roll in the national newspapers is now indistinguishable from *Hot Press*. The culture has flipped over, and the meaning of the revolution has inverted itself without anyone noticing.

Every generation, as George Orwell observed, imagines itself to be more intelligent than the one that went before it, and wiser than the one that comes after it. This is a healthy state of affairs, causing the young to interrogate the certainties and achievements of their elders, and then tender their own solutions to society's ageless questions. The clash of energies between young and old, the tug-of-war between rebels and establishment, creates a forward dynamic that is, to an extent, self-purifying, self-adjusting and self-regulating. The national blackboard is accessible to anyone with the impulse and nerve to erase what has become accepted conventional wisdom, and chalk out a better way. Ideas get tested and thereby made stronger; establishments are never allowed to get too secure; the dialectic between opposing visions enables well-tested solutions to have the best chance of success. But, in Ireland, we experience a problem – and somewhat more acutely than it is experienced elsewhere – because of how this process has been subverted by the presence of the Peter Pan generation at the heart of our affairs. Some time in the past generation, this natural order of challenge and succession ceased to function. A set of ideas was written on the national blackboard that nobody sought to wipe off. The young began to lose interest in the discussion, to become, as was so frequently lamented, 'apathetic'. In the discussions that have taken place about why this has occurred, the tendency has been to focus on the young. What is wrong with them? Why do they lack civic spirit? Where is their attitude of naive and ignorant rebellion? What do they believe in? It has not yet occurred to anyone that the problem may be elsewhere, that it may lie, not with the young who have withdrawn, but with the middle-aged who have embezzled the national bank of youth.

Peter Pan syndrome has infected every political culture in the West. Its symptoms have been rather scarily outlined in Robert Bly's remarkable analysis of 'the sibling society', in which he depicts the modern generations of half-adults pummelling hysterically at the chests of their fathers, berating their failures and calling them fascists. Bly paints a devastating portrait of a society obsessed by youth, suspicious of any form of authority that seeks to deprive it of its 'freedoms', intent upon destroying its own inheritance of what he calls 'vertical' culture, in favour of the 'horizontal' culture of its peer generation – pop music, movies, television and a limited range of books which relate to these other contemporary media much more than to any literary or artistic heritage recognizable as such.

But this youth-obsession is not held by the young – rather, it is clung to by a generation born midway through the last century, which became so addicted to rebellion and irresponsibility that, even though ensconced in power now for several decades, it refuses to hand on the baton of youth to those with whom it properly belongs. Politically, the Peter Pan generation clings to the idea of a rolling frontier of libertarianism – without limits, costs or consequences. Never having confronted the untenabilities of its own irresponsibility, it has no concept of the vital importance of authority. It is intoxicated with its own love of freedom, which it perceives only in terms of what it has insolently won from its parent-generation, forgetting that this had before, in Ireland and elsewhere, been bought with blood. And, never asking where its freedoms came from, it never pauses to wonder who will protect them if they again come under threat. It has rejected all heavenly and earthly establishments and, though now itself in power, still wants to affect the appearance of rebellion and wear flowers in its hair. The Peter Pan generation, though now burdened with responsibilities of its own, and in some instances with responsibility for the safety of the world, insists on perceiving everything in terms of the corruption and dereliction of previous generations. In power, it refuses to take unpopular decisions, determined to be liked above all. It seeks to inhabit the corridors of power and public office without exercising authority, and feels free to excoriate its forebears precisely because of the preparedness of past generations to say 'No' when necessary, to ask for the postponement of gratification when appropriate, and to endure unpopularity in the interests of the greater good.

The natural growth and development of any society demands a process of renunciation by the mature, which in turn requires at its back a strong, safe, generous agent to act as buffer and punchbag. There, in the old society, my father and his generation once stood. But the Peter Pan generation utterly repudiates such a notion in favour of a woolly correctness that offends no one. The result, in the phrase of the German psychotherapist Alexander Mitscherlich, borrowed by Bly for the title of his book, *The Sibling Society*, is 'a gigantic army of rival, envious siblings'. Sibling society has no time for glory, or effort or justice, or greatness, or duty, or patriotism, but is content with consumer durables, celebrity and shallow forms of freedom. Liberalism has become a badge of valour and enlightenment, prohibiting public self-interrogation. And the most prized idea of the Peter Pan generation is that it is the Most Liberal Generation Ever.'

Although the language of the political discourse maintained under the direction of the Peter Pans persistently conveys a strong sense that the people advocating these positions have high hopes of one day overturning the present establishment and bringing their enlightenment to the dark corners of the system, the truth is that they are already ensconced in the system, and have been for years. As a result of Peter Pan Syndrome, Irish society at the start of the twenty-first century finds itself paralysed by neurosis, denial and lack of self-knowledge, its corridors of power haunted by the ghosts of an establishment which, though long since departed from power and the flesh, remains a central element of the public imagination, because the real inhabitants of the citadels of power are refusing to admit that they are now the establishment. The most immediate and worrying symptom of this – aside from perennial boredom with the repetitiveness of public debate – is that the dynamic of public conversation is not provided by the tension between the young and old of the present, but continues to be dominated by a noisy squabble between the middle-aged of the present and the long-departed dinosaurs of the twentieth century. We find ourselves, in Ireland in 2007, at the tail-end of a grotesquely extended debate between the revolutionary generation of the 1960s and the establishment which that generation – rightly, by any objective assessment – indicted for its stewardship of Ireland in the first half-century of independence. Today, even as the age we live in poses ever more challenging questions about globalism, mass immigration, terrorism, neo-poverty, collapsing forms of collective identity, and ever more subtle forms of totalitarianism, Ireland continues its war with 'traditional' Catholicism, with de Valera and the Christian Brothers, with Fianna Fáil's allegedly insular version of national identity, and with anyone who once sought to place limits on the freedoms of those who were young a generation ago.

The values of the Peter Pan generation include an opposition to war, regardless of morality; a belief in personal freedom unabashed by the contradiction that this cannot be defined other than relative to the freedoms of others; a belief in 'social justice' for the down-trodden, coupled with a desire for a low-tax economy; a commitment to theoretical alternativism, except when the outcome of this is likely to cause discomfort to the believer; a belief in equality, other than for unapproved groups, such as, in different contexts, men, whites, straights and conservatives; a hatred of America, especially when the Republican Party is in power; an entrenched opposition to organized religions, other than those emanating from the East; a belief in the moral unassailability of certain named victimologies which, having been approved by the Peter Pan ideology, have acquired total legitimacy – these include women, black people, homosexuals, travellers, children in contexts where they are deemed to belong to women, refugees, immigrants, asylum seekers, and the women and children of war zones in places where the Peter Pans have withheld approval for the war. But perhaps the most pervasive idea of the Peter Pan generation is that God, because he had been foisted upon them by a generation they came to despise, should be abolished.

One of the difficulties besetting the capacity of religion to confront the nature of the modern world is connected to language: how it is used and who controls it. Religions have their own languages, which believers speak among themselves, though each of these languages has more in common with others than is often acknowledged. Believers the world over speak broadly the same language of piety, austerity and devotion. But their communications with the outside world are necessarily limited, or doomed to be misunderstood.

The problem is not so much with secularism as with the public language which has evolved in tandem with it. The language of the public domain, under the influence of the Peter Pan mindset, is not so much actively hostile to religious ideas as imbued with a deep fear of them, which frequently causes the message of religion to be misstated and therefore misunderstood.

Under the influence of the pseudo-rebelliousness of the Peter Pans, our age is unremittingly cynical about both the idea of God and the possibility of belief. Belief, where it exists, is regarded with embarrassment or scepticism, as though it represents a defect of personality, excusable only by dint of extreme experience or vested interest. In the postmodern age, God is as much a stain on the public identities of believers as sin was once upon the souls of the faithful. It is not simply that God has become unfashionable, but that our need to feel in control of our world has caused us to make Him redundant. Belief in God has been designated as a mark of backwardness – at best condescended to, and more often regarded with disdain and derision. The age of hyper-rationality has rendered God unfashionable and embarrassing, and the result is that the godless hordes have lost the horizon which might have made modern life more liveable. We have an extreme difficulty in acknowledging the probability that human beings have an inbuilt need, individually and collectively, to draw a chalk line around their knowledge and control of the world, and to hand over control of much of what they themselves cannot manage to a higher being or force. In the absence of a collectively recognized God, the individual is cast back on his own imaginative resources to perceive this higher order in his own way. Hence, the epidemic of alternativism that has followed the announcement of God's demise. But this, being fragmented and isolating, has limited usefulness for either the collective or, ultimately, the individual.

Virtually every mention of God in the public space of our modern societies is interpreted within an established model of thought which is difficult to circumnavigate. We see God as a kind of establishment presence, a forbidding force demanding obedience, respect and adoration. Thus, any attempt to invoke His name invites a backlash from those who have set their caps against either God or the very possibility of God, which includes not just atheists and agnostics but also those who believe in God but just don't like Him very much. It is assumed that, by invoking God, an advocate of spiritual inquiry must perforce be trying to persuade people to resubmit themselves to an authority they have either dismissed or repudiated.

The Irish experience of these quintessentially postmodern conditions has its roots in the social context in which power was transferred from the last truly 'grown-up' generation of Irish politicians, which began to vacate the stage from the late 1950s. You might also define this generation as the last not to have to deal with the incessant public conversation created and nurtured by wall-to-wall media. The most overwhelming, and ironically least remarked-upon influence of mass media was the placing of the youth agenda centre stage, and the first generation to feel the benefits of this have been unwilling to let go of the benefits and move aside in the way that nature intended. The benefit of mass media as a conduit of youthful energies has been a one-off affair, unavailable to subsequent generations, who now resort to atomizing media like mobile telephones and internet chatrooms to communicate with one another.

At the core of this process has occurred a distortion of the meaning of idealism, which might also be described as the expression of the uncontaminated longing of the human being. Idealism is not the prerogative of the young, but cannot exist anywhere if it is not felt by those with most of their lives in front of them. The young, having no responsibility for the present or the future, are free to challenge and revolt, to repudiate and scorn the efforts and contributions of those who preceded them. This is entirely natural and healthy, being an essential element not merely of the growth of individuals but of the testing and strengthening of a society. The problems begin when the baton of idealism is not handed down. Firstly, this affects the way in which idealism itself is perceived. When radical thoughts and disturbing emotions are directed not at the actually existing imperfections of the present but at the fossilized grievances of the past, there develops in society a sense that idealism, rather than a pure energy, is actually an ideology belonging to a particular faction. When this happens, the innate irrefutability of the moral authority of youthful anger becomes suspect, by virtue of the inescapable moral relativity of the concerns being expressed which, having come adrift from the energy of youth, mutate into conduits of something approaching hysteria. Put another way: there are things which young people should want and demand, because they are attractive to the young, but this does not mean that they are always objectively and absolutely beneficial. There is no longer a filter in the public consciousness capable of exercising or advising discretion in this regard. By the same token, there are things that young people want and desire that are expressions of the most sacred dimensions of the human personality, but these, similarly, remain unexpressed because the channels of idealistic expression have been usurped.

We know, for example, from a host of indicators, that Irish society has a profound and growing problem with its young men. These indicators include road accident statistics, binge-drinking and suicide by teenage boys and young males. Some years ago I attended a fascinating lecture in Dublin by the American Franciscan priest Father Richard Rohr, about young men in the modern world. Father Rohr, with a nod or two towards another seminal book, by the great American poet and writer Robert Bly, *Iron John*, which talked about rites of passage, about recreating a tradition of initiation by which young men could be affirmed in their manhood, and about the damaging way in which men had become over-feminized – not just in our education systems, though this was so, but in the entire culture of Western society, including Christianity. We had destroyed, he said, the transformative energies which men respect, which serve to connect young men to the mystical source of existence, to awaken them to pain and powerlessness, and to usher them safely over the threshold into manhood. Women have, or had until recently, less need of such initiation, because the idea of motherhood provides a strong coherent meaning for girls, who also have a clear and painful moment of entry into womanhood. Men require this moment to be culturally supplied by their fathers and the male elders of their communities, the ones who know where the journey leads.

Concerning the horrendous levels of road carnage involving young men, I once wrote about how Gay Byrne, the former broadcaster and chairman of the Road Traffic Association, painted a graphic picture of driving in Donegal. You would be driving along a country road, he said, when up ahead you would see a car bouncing towards you at speed. You prayed the young male driver would be able to maintain control until he had passed you by. Contemplating this image, I was struck by the idea that there might be a comparison between our out-of-control male driver and the suicide bomber in some Muslim cultures. The context is different, but they seem both to be expressions of a perversion, a short-circuiting of meaning.

Whereas Islamic societies tend to maintain a strictly one-dimensional view of the relationship between tradition and modern reality, Irish society has surrendered to a multi-dimensional, unstructured and rootless attitude. The Peter Pan-dominated society of modern Ireland has disparaged and discarded tradition, leaving the young with nothing to challenge them, nothing to compare themselves with, nothing even to fight.

Ideally, a child needs to grow up in a coherent tradition which, while transmitting its own principles with love and conviction, is open enough to enable the testing of its value system against others. The element in Islamic cultures provoking the emergence of the fundamentalist extremist appears to be the rigidity of the tradition and its poor adaptability to different forms of reality. When Islamic culture is transplanted into a secularized, hyper-liberal environment, a host of complexes are created in the minds of some youngsters, who react by plunging deep into the tradition.

Our culture is, in a sense, the opposite. Having recently emerged from rigid tradition into a virtual free-for-all, we have replaced our former insistence on the conveyance of a singular notion of meaning with a pick-and-mix culture in which the child is left struggling to comprehend reality, his idealism short-circuiting into a public culture which, while lionizing youth, in reality seeks to ape, replicate and perpetuate its characteristics and concerns. This syndrome, for the reasons already outlined, and also because maleness has become a suspect characteristic in the ideology of modern Ireland, bears down on males more than females. The signals picked up by the young man tell him that he may find his meaning and identity as an entrepreneur, a sportsman or a plumber. But, because he is primed with questions that go far deeper than business, sport or plumbing, this explodes in him an extreme reaction not dissimilar in psychological terms to the reaction of the young Muslim man who, unable to reconcile the external culture with what he has been taught, dives backwards for reassurance into the deepest parts of the tradition. The young Irishman, lacking this option, plunges forward in a hedonistic rush, and, because he walks on the Peter Pan-created quicksand, speeds up to stay above ground. The two, the young Irishman and the young Muslim, are equally out of control, but seek different ways to answer back. One straps himself around with explosives and walks into a city. The other, perhaps less consciously, gets behind a steering wheel, puts the pedal to the metal and explodes onto a country road.

Meanwhile, the demands of youth have become as fetishes of a form of pseudo-idealism that infects every aspect of public thought and conversation. It often seems, to those who are not wholly affected by this condition, and most especially to the genuinely young, that idealistic causes are merely offensive weapons, existing to enhance the moral standing of the accusers and diminish those whom they accuse. Commentators who live comfortable lives, without any visible evidence of sacrifice or Christian charity, berate the rest of society for its failure to value the 'underprivileged'. Everyone knows that this is a pretence, but nobody talks about it, because to do so would invite splenetic accusation and moralistic condemnation. This corrupts the very language of idealism, making it impossible any longer to find uncontaminated words with which to express fine feelings or ambitions, rendering innocence indistinguishable from cynicism, and leaving the genuinely young and potentially truly idealistic at a loss for public words and feelings to express social, political or spiritual longings. In these circumstances, idealism becomes an illusion, a matter of words which inspire only the converted and disappoint even them. This renders the young literally speechless, unable to identify with much that is expressed, and totally unconvinced by the energy they feel from the discussion. Young people need to own their rebellions, not in any psychotherapeutic sense, but in the very precise and practical sense of needing to feel that their outrage, their desire, their questioning, belongs to them. If those they should be outraged against seem to be more outraged than they are, confusion reigns. And when the pubic forum is dominated by cynicism, it is all but impossible to find a channel by which to articulate something genuinely idealistic or naive. What the young feel in their hearts becomes inexpressible, because, even as the issues that concern them go unspoken in public, the language and passion that is necessary for their articulation is already being mimicked in public discourse. There seems to be no place in the public realm into which the young can themselves move, and no language in which they can express themselves. In Ireland, this, yes, betrayal, has been more pronounced than elsewhere, because the appropriation of idealism occurred not just for the normal reasons; that is to say the, in some ways, quite natural reluctance of maturing people to admit that they are no longer as young or as radical as they were – but also because a particular element within the Irish political spectrum perceived that Irish reality offered the means by which it could, by commandeering the franchise on rebellion, hold power indefinitely on the basis that it spoke with the voice of youth. Because of the particular circumstances prevailing in Ireland – the failures of previous hegemonies, including religious, nationalistic and political – a space was created wherein forces which claimed to be opposing these past tyrannies could build a new establishment without seeming to do so.

Everything is upside down. The language of rebellion has been hijacked and the iconography of youth turned into a grotesque parody which, in truth, celebrates not youth but the sad spectacle of old people trying to deny both gravity and reality. Attitudes, energies and activities once rightly considered to be the province of the young are now embraced by the middle-aged and older, and even sometimes by the very people whom, theoretically, these attitudes, energies and activities should properly be directed against.

I had already written the gist of this chapter in April 2005 when I read in the newspaper about a speech by the then Josef Cardinal Ratzinger in advance of the conclave to decide who should succeed the recently deceased John Paul II as pope. 'We are moving', declared the cardinal, toward 'a dictatorship of relativism . . . that recognizes nothing definite and leaves only one's own ego and one's own desires as the final measure.' The modern world, Ratzinger insisted, has jumped 'from one extreme to the other: from Marxism to liberalism, up to libertinism; from collectivism to radical individualism; from atheism to a vague religious mysticism; from agnosticism to syncretism and on and on.' The newspaper report recalled that Ratzinger had earlier in his career been a moderate, if not a liberal, but had developed a mistrust of the left following the student revolts in his native Germany during the 1960s. These revolutions, he had said, 'turned into a radical attack on human freedom and dignity, a deep threat to all that is human'. Had I simply read this statement in its reported context, I would not have understood it, and might well have dismissed it as the prejudice of an elderly man, but having struggled for some time to produce a sketch of the social context in which I myself had drifted away from faith, it made absolute sense.

The obsession with youth in the present era in the West is the most intense the world has ever seen. At its heart is a fear of death, itself a symptom of loss of faith. Because our generations have no true belief in a hereafter, all our hopes hinge on the realization of our appetites in the only existence we know about. The idea that our lives might pass and leave us still full of longing is one that terrifies us to where our very souls used to be. Our societies tell us that our chances of happiness depend on the number (our chronological age) we carry around in our heads, just behind our faces, keeping us ever more awake as fear of the ultimate sleep encroaches. All the time we seek an unattainable perfection, waiting to freeze-frame ourselves in that optimal moment when we think we have it.

One of the devices which a neurotically advancing society employs to protect its flawed prospectus is the idea of perpetually unrolling perfection: thanks to the enlightened agenda being promoted by the invisible establishment, things are, every day, in every way, getting better and better. The counterpoint to this is the idea of a reactionary recalcitrance on the part of those who, by virtue of underdeveloped consciousness, refuse to believe in the perfection project. Usually this tussle occurs between youth and age, but in Ireland, as we've seen, it takes place between different parts of the same head, an old part and a young part, and this erupts in the public domain as a struggle between progress and tradition, or, as we depict it in Ireland, between liberalism and conservatism. For a generation now, the liberal ethic has been in the ascendant, climbing into the consciousness of Western society, preaching freedom, tolerance, individualism, libertarianism and equality. Until recently, this ethic had been unchallengeable, because it flew in the face of what seemed to be an unrepentant and unflappable conservatism, which anyone with even a few red corpuscles must delight in doing down. Drawing primarily on the energy generated in the 1960s by rock 'n' roll and the sexual revolution, this ethic thrived on being outside the mainstream, on its oppositional mission and its rejection of staidness, prudery and greyness. I understand the Peter Pan mentality because I suffer from it. Only through necessity have I started to examine and interrogate it within myself.

It is a visceral as well as an intellectual condition. The idea of, in middle age, 'becoming reactionary' or 'turning conservative', is horrifying for most of us who were born in the second half of the twentieth century. There is something physically repulsive about the very notion of conservatism. To talk about God is embarrassing to the point of seizure. To acknowledge authority is a betrayal of weakness. We associate these values, ideas, phenomena, with people who wear out-of-date clothes, and sport exaggeratedly bushy eyebrows and dandruff on their collars. They are to us the return, not of the repressed, but the repressors, those who tried to control us and limit our freedoms.

About fifteen years ago, I was in the home of a noted Irish conservative politician, waiting for the result of a crucial referendum to do with abortion. Things were not going well for the conservatives and the news coming through on the telephone, radio and television was uniformly bad. I had been detailed to spend the day with the politician and register his responses, but I was there under protest, because in truth I was a bit terrified of his reputation. I imagined having to watch my language, stifle my yawns and bite my lip as we pulled into the hard shoulder to say the angelus. In fact, he was a deeply engaging man, full of fun and mischief. As we drove around through the day he regaled me with hair-raising stories of his early life of boozing, womanizing and destruction. He had drunk several of the family businesses and all but destroyed his health in the process. He told me too about his moment of epiphany, which had nothing to do with angels or forked lightning, but occurred one night when, at a loss for something to read, he picked up one of his son's Superman comics. I wish I could remember the details of the story that so moved him, because he told me that he never looked back. Now, as the gloomy news of his defeat came through, he paused momentarily between the phone and the television and broke into a spontaneous dance, accompanying himself with a ditty

'diddled' in the disturbingly familiar Irish style. He danced about for
a bit and then smartly clicked his heels and bowed. I think it was at
that moment that I began to rethink my notions about conservatism.

There is a conventional view, at least as prevalent in Ireland as in
other Western societies, that conservatism is something that, generally speaking, descends with middle age, usually as the expression of
a desire to hold on to status and possessions as much as values and
ideas. People, by this logic, become conservative as they grow older
because they have something to lose. They begin to fear death, to
consider the possibility of an afterlife. The implication of this logic
is that belief in a hereafter is predicated on fear. The positions of
the old, therefore, are presented as self-serving, opportunistic and
morally dubious.

There may come a time soon in Ireland when it is possible to
suggest that the reason 'conservative' views are usually expressed by
older people is that, when you've been around long enough with an
open mind, you tend to see things in a broader perspective and know
the values of what is in danger of being lost. Perhaps the initiative
will come from parents, who perceive the dangers to their children
from the very ideas which they themselves adopted and promoted
while themselves young. Because our era seems to value youth above
all other qualities, it has become difficult to insert into public discussion anything that seems to counsel caution or postponement or
moderation, or in any way to run against the youthful desire for total
freedom in all things. To outline the possible risks of an imbalance
between freedom and responsibility is immediately identified as a
reactionary response. The result is that the media, which act as the
conduit of our discussions, have become dominated by a view which
seeks in all things to pander to what is perceived to be the natural
position of the young, to the promotion of a narrow sense of
freedom and a blinkered set of values based on individualism and
immediacy. Pseudo-liberalism, denying that it is now the absolute
ruler of all things, pursues a war against a defeated opponent, issuing
from the citadels of power its daily bulletins implying that the battle
has not yet been won. A phantom enemy, inspired by forces long
banished or dead, is placed before the people, lest their anger abate
and good sense return. The values which a generation ago were

regarded as extreme and unthinkable have now become the formal values of our age, and secretly we are just as dissatisfied with these new values as we were with the old ones. In place of the old rigidities is a new set of orthodoxies, formed as the negative images of that which has been routed. So it is, for example, that heterosexual marriage can no longer be regarded as a norm of society, or at least as any more elevated than any other union of choice, since this would be to discriminate against minorities or offend their sensitivities. Or, similarly, not only can educational standards no longer be imposed on those who find them restrictive, but they must be abolished to avoid preferential treatment of those who excelled in the old order. Many people do not express views on these phenomena, because they know that behind them lurks an ideology far more intolerant than anything it claims to oppose.

But perhaps, in our heart of hearts, some of us allow ourselves to wonder where it is all going to end. Perhaps we have a sense that it has gone beyond issues of tolerance, equality and individual freedom, and has become something else. For sometimes it seems that what began as a youthful desire to destabilize intolerance, rigidity and hypocrisy has, by virtue perhaps of its immunity to the interrogation of age, drifted away from any kind of moorings in wisdom or commonsense. The liberal ethic, having fulfilled its mission, has failed to self-collapse, and so it runs virulently on, like a genetically modified weed. And since it is refusing to self-collapse, it is inevitable that it will seek to collapse, instead, the norms of the society in which it now lingers like a virus.

This mindset infects our collective capacity to engage with the idea of God. He ticks all the wrong boxes. For most of us He is still an old man with a long white beard, humourless, severe, part of the establishment, an embarrassing reminder of former subservience and lack of freedom. But a change is gonna come. In the next couple of decades, Ireland will move from having a predominantly youthful population to a predominantly middle-aged and elderly population. This will usher in profound changes in public culture and put up for grabs many of the sacred cows of the past generation. Age is one of the great tyrannies of our time, not so much because of its ineluctable attrition as our absolute inability to accept it. My parents' generation seemed to go through the stages of life with something approaching acceptance, relating to, rather than competing with each other, seeking balance between youth and experience and seeming to be more connected to some constant essence of themselves than to the meaning of the numbers on their foreheads. But the Peter Pan obsession with ageing causes us to miss youth, including relative youth, as we cling to an edifice of our own creation, as though by doing so we could achieve eternity of our own volition. People, generally, are living longer than ever, but grow exponentially more miserable about being older. There should be some comfort in togetherness, but there is only the loneliness born of mutual terror, communicated mainly in the avoidance of the subject. Though half the pages of any newspaper tell us we're counting from the wrong end, our fear of growing old prevents us from realizing that we're as young as we're ever going to be, and acting on the implications. The ultimate irony of all this is that the generations now about to unleash that senior explosion are those that, in the second half of the last century, worked so hard to undermine the authority and alleged privilege of age. For the botox-treadmill-Viagra generations, youth was all. We imagined we would be young forever, blind to the certainty that, by indulging our prejudiced view of age and ageing, we were thickening a fog of prejudice that now lies waiting for us. The flower children have stigmatized their finally grown-up selves.

But we may be approaching an interesting moment in the struggle that has monopolized public discussions in Ireland and elsewhere for a generation: the moment, long anticipated but much delayed, when the momentum of liberalism and rational scepticism will have exhausted itself. Right now, we seem to be at the end of the era which began with the arrival of Garret FitzGerald, half a lifetime ago. Not only are we emerging from our short burst of tigerish prosperity, into God knows what, but it is beginning to appear that the long-standing agenda of individual freedom and interrogation of traditional forms of authority may have finally run its course. Nobody seems to know what to do next, but there is a growing awareness that some direction needs to be found or the future will declare itself against our wishes. It is rapidly becoming clearer that what we need right now from politics is not broad-brush social change, but refinements and adjustments on changes already implemented, and there are countless contexts of Irish life where such initiatives are necessary and possible, without major implications for the progress already achieved. There is an urgent necessity for a moral social vision which might help to reorientate our collective concept of the purpose of social life. More specifically, there is a sense that the values of individualism and personal freedom have infected social thought, policy and institutions to such an extent that there is no longer any collective sense of what social values should properly encompass. At the back of all these issues lurks the spectre of what we know as religion.

# — 3 —

# Georgie

In our lifetimes, the ubiquity of illusion began with the promise of the sixties, which came out of the dark, a promise of liberation from the gloom of conservatism, respectability and greyness. The message was: it needn't be like this; freedom is within reach. But life is a fragile condition existing between two kinds of death: the grey death of respectability and the literal death the adventurous seek to defy. Human happiness requires a fund of dreams, but also something countervailing: balance, restraint, an understanding that the ecstatic promise, because it delivers to a point and then starts to destroy, is duplicitous.

When I was a child in primary school, we did what we called 'projects'. These generally involved a variant on the essay, with some kind of pictorial dimension, perhaps a few coloured photos from a magazine glued into a scrapbook and elaborated with painfully extended text. The only one I can remember with any clarity was one I called 'God or Supergod?', a treatise on the connection, or perhaps tension, between God and George Best. I must admit that, even as I was making it, I regarded the connection as tenuous, but since then I have become less sure.

The story of the late George Best offers us a telling fable of the nature of dreams and the limits of illusion. George was, on the surface of things, a marginal symbol of the sixties revolution. By one reading he slipstreamed on the flower-power dream that blossomed from the rock 'n' roll beat, a stowaway on the movement created by the Beatles, Stones, Elvis, Dylan and the Doors. But this is to see only haircuts and clothes, the dream as mere spectacle. By this analysis, George adopted the fashions of his time and became a shining star in a medium not previously noted for colour or flamboyance. This is the 'tragic' story of George Best: how his adoption of counter-culture values would lead to the restlessness that clung to him throughout his short, spectacular life. The 'moral' of this story is that, had he kept his hair short and his eye on the ball, he would have been good for several more decades.

There are other ways of seeing it. I became aware of George in the late 1960s, not yet in my teens. I encountered him first in the newspapers, but for a while got him mixed up with George Harrison. We didn't have TV, never mind *Match of the Day*, but I would see flashes of his drop-dead genius on screens in other people's houses. I didn't have much to compare him with, but saw instantly that he was incomparable. Anyone who saw him play, if only for a moment, was liberated from greyness, if only for a while. Even before I knew the sixties had started, his every move said: 'Freedom!'

Best was my first hero, to the point of obsession. I grew my hair to look like him and tried unsuccessfully to get nicknamed 'Georgie'. My scrapbooks of his dribblings and doings caused familial concerns about testosterone depletion. A briefly charting record of a song called 'Georgie' by Don Fardon, the most nondescript of records, became the first I ever bought.

A couple of years before George Best died in 2005, as his rapid decline unfolded in full view of the world, I came across a book in a second-hand bookshop that made me weep. It was a photographic biography of Georgie, full of pictures of him at his sublime, impossibly handsome prime, playing on the field and off, posing with his beautiful house, sitting in sleek soft-tops with the most awe-inspiring women in the world.

When first I saw him play, in that European Cup encounter with Benfica, my life changed. The reception was bad, and the game seemed to be played in a mist, from which occasionally this dark figure would emerge, running like a greyhound and turning like a ballerina, leaving a detritus of spread-eagled bodies behind him. There was something superhuman in the way he played, something unworldly and yet transcendent in both the worldly and theological senses. He did things that seemed both awesome and pointless – as though to demonstrate that the impossible was within reach. Only those flickering bits of footage serve to reassure us that George Best was not a dream. When you haven't watched it for a while, you forget, lose faith in its ethereal qualities, think you have imagined it or fallen foul of hyperbole or wishful thinking. And then, your breath is taken again. In a world where exaggeration is the authorized form of mass communication, George Best remained understated. He was better than it is possible for human minds to imagine. The perennial discussions – Giggsy or Bestie? Becks or Bestie? Keano or Bestie? – are just tabloid space-fillers. Even Pelé, the closest anyone has come, put the matter to bed in a word. 'Best,' he said in response to that perennial question. It was not false modesty: Pelé was a better footballer, team player, all-rounder, but Best's genius started where Pelé's ended – at the beginning of the impossible. There are few things one can, with confidence, lay before a new generation and say, 'There! That was what inspired me.' Just as Buddy Holly means nothing to anyone who takes the Beatles for granted, most things we remember as precursors are meaningless to generations inoculated with sensation. But there is one word I have heard more often than any other from the mouths of those watching those misty images for the first time, and that word is 'Jesus!' It is never a profanity. His 'genius', as it was rightly called, involved the salutary demonstration of existential defiance, of individual triumph over those who make up the numbers. His existence seemed to say that if you discover your own secrets, you can become a god while still walking the earth.

Though the sixties thing is regarded now as primarily a rock 'n' roll revolution, it wasn't until punk that rock 'n' roll did what George had been doing with a football a decade before. As much a prophet as Lennon or Jagger, what made him special was that, unlike the rock 'n' rollers, he commanded a medium we instantly understood and could immediately access as participants. The music of the Beatles or the Stones inspired us, but did not yet invite us to be active in our own liberation. You could dream about being Lennon or McCartney, but, without a recording studio and a George Martin, couldn't actually become one.

By growing your hair, you could, however, be George Best. All you needed was a rood of space and a couple of jumpers to mark the goals. In a few objectively ungainly spurts through the mud, the dream would come alive. To an onlooker you might be a skinny cub with shaggy locks and unconvincing sideburns, but in the cocoon of the spell you had reached a place beyond dreams. George was a Pied Piper whose life became for his followers not a means to explore their fantasies vicariously, but a way into their own potential. In those moments in which you clung to the ball as though to your life, you accessed a sense of what might be possible – beyond football, music, anything.

The true moral in the life of George Best has something to do with the simultaneous indispensability and limits of dreams, and the para-doxical nature of freedom. He was a god-turned-man. There were other kinds of freedom he might have found for himself and been saved, had he not glimpsed so much of the life of the gods. But he set us free, and not in a small way, while himself succumbing to the tragedy that offers us both a warning and a map. His life and death tell us anything is possible, but at a price. The world hasn't enough space for everyone's dreams, and, when you are a dream-maker like George, those whom you inspired, but who failed to score for themselves, will return to suck you dry, to prove to themselves that your feet, like theirs, are made of dirt. In the end, the ghouls will, if you let them, define you, and towards the end George found himself at their mercy.

As I grew older and underwent my own crucifixion at the mercy of alcohol, I began to watch George Best even more closely than I had as a teenager. I began to feel like he was part of me, like a residual fantasy that sought to trick me into believing it had come true. There was a time when I felt utter despair at the idea that I could never be like him, that I had been cheated by birth to live out an ordinary life when I felt that the life of a god was my entitlement. There were times, later on, when I felt a tawdry sense of *Schadenfreude* that I, at least, had managed to preserve myself from the ignominy of this spectacular experiment. But always, for nearly 30 years, I watched Georgie's trajectory with feelings that went far beyond the voyeuris-tic. In a sense, he was me and I him. He was living my life as I might have wished it to be, and I was watching him burn out spectacularly.

We shake our heads about the tragedy of George Best: how he got waylaid by money and women and drink, how he had it all and threw it all away. But I don't know. I mourned when he left Manchester United, but perhaps he knew that there's a point beyond which repetition risks rendering the supernatural banal. It's easy to fall into platitude about what he was 'doing to himself', but the true mystery was: what kept him alive when he was no longer a god? George Best tried Alcoholics Anonymous several times, but it didn't take. 'How can George Best be anonymous?' he would ask with a shrug. But there was, of course, a more profound problem. The programme of AA promises 'a life beyond your wildest dreams', and it is hardly necessary to labour the nature of the problem this represented for George.

For mortals, there is hope of relief: you can restore the shattered illusions with new ones, earthly or otherwise. But what when your dreams are behind you, when you have been to Camelot already? And how do you propose a spiritual awakening to one who knows, as you do, that he has walked in the skin of a god?

# — 4 —

# The Unquenchable Thirst

When I was young I used to ask the most fundamental questions all
the time. What am I? Who made me (sometimes, though not always,
in the sense of Who is this God Who made me)? What am I doing
here? Why now rather than a million years ago? Was there always a
'now' or is the present nowness just a trick of my presence? Was I
always present in one form or another? Will I be present after I die?
Where, physically, might heaven be?

I had lots of 'smaller' questions too. Why did Jesus need to die for
me? In what sense did He do this? Since He knew what was going to
happen, and also that He would rise again, how could it be called a
sacrifice?

When I became what I in retrospect describe as an 'agnostic',
these questions vanished from my consciousness. Occasionally I
would trot them out in order to argue with someone who asserted a
belief in God, but for myself they were no longer live questions.
This suggests to me that my 'agnosticism' was never an actual
position, but rather an evasion. Reacting to the dark spectre of
Catholicism, I withdrew, not into a new and convinced philosophical position, but into a kind of self-constructed box which shut out
questions that seemed, to my consciousness then, irrelevant. Perhaps
this is a tendency that goes with young adulthood. Children are alive
to these questions because they are opening up to reality and are still
overawed by its possibilities. Older people return to these questions
for entirely different reasons. But in between, perhaps from late
teens through to late middle age, the average citizen of modern
society tends to airbrush these questions out of sight. There is a life
to be led, an economy to participate in, work to be done, fun to
be had.

71

Another way of putting this would be to say that, from the time I became an adult until I arrived at my forties, I avoided serious consideration of the fundamental meanings of things. I constructed a box for myself and lived within it, allowing the logic of the world to supply all my answers. This is not difficult for an adult in a modern society, because so much of reality is prefabricated, sterile and safe. There is risk, fear, of course, but these can be kept at bay also, by artificial means. Art, which used to have a role in society intimately bound up with religion, nowadays serves to insulate the boxes of the middle-aged evaders from the incursion of reality. It deals, of course, with the fundamental things, but in a compartmentalized way that renders them distant and safe. Like a cultural inoculation, it immunizes the citizen against the implications of anything beyond their prefabricated reality. It is, after all, 'Art', which, having its own page in the newspaper, signifies a discipline designed to elevate intelligent people, albeit in a manageable and, where possible, rational way.

To be an agnostic, then, is to enter a landscaped reality which continually tells us that it is the totality of reality. It is to forget what life is, while remaining convinced that you are still in touch with reality.

Thus did I live for more than twenty years. I had tidied the big questions out of my view and was getting on with enjoying myself.

It didn't at the time, or indeed for a long time afterwards, strike me that there was any particular connection between my taking up drinking and my letting go of religion. If you'd put it to me, I'd have called it a coincidence, or connected the two events only in the sense of both being symptoms of growing up. But now, after many years of thinking about it, I have no doubt that these were not two events, but one. I abandoned one form of spirituality, the kind that sat on a fluffy cloud in the sky, for another that came in bottles. I gave up God and took up the glass. For alcohol is a kind of higher power, one of a growing number that modern people need to ensure that their prefabricated boxes remain impervious to the encroachment of larger realities.

People think of drink largely as a social lubricant, a means for them to relax and be more 'themselves'. But its function as relaxant, de-inhibitor, is something of a distraction. It is, fundamentally, a mind-altering substance. As well as repressing the layers of social conditioning which serve to police our behaviour, it opens up a previously undreamt-of inner universe of creativity, imagination, freedom and joy. Beyond this, because there is no free ride in this world, and because ethyl alcohol is a poison, this chemical facilitator of artificial serenity begins to eat away at the souls of those whose need to preserve their denial of reality requires more and more concentrated doses.

I was born shy. As a child, I was a loner who, suffering from a chronic form of bronchitis, spent most of my time at home in bed reading. As a teenager I spread my wings a little, playing a bit of soccer and taking an interest in pop music, but I remained tongue-tied and prone to profound panic when in the company of strangers, especially girls to whom I was even slightly attracted.

This changed about halfway down my second pint of Smithwicks. In Ballaghadereen one night in the late summer of 1973, I had a couple of pints with Gerry Byrne, who had been my best friend from infants' class, and who had given me both my first guitar and my first guitar lesson. Then Gerry and I headed for the Midnight Club. Gerry was already a seasoned drinker, although three months younger than me. I still remember the sense of exhilaration that accompanied me on the walk from the hotel bar to the dance hall: it was as though I was floating two feet above the ground. I felt no shyness, no inhibition. I had discovered a way of making myself whole. Although I had been going to dances for a while, I danced that night more than I had ever danced before. I talked and laughed with girls. I even 'squared', which is how we described getting off with someone, which back then meant simply walking them home and maybe kissing round a corner from their front door. After this I 'rested' from alcohol for nearly a year, half terrified at my discovery, half conscious that I had found an 'answer' to nearly all my problems. I was to resume in earnest following the night in the early summer of 1974 when I met those older friends on my way to confession.

My relationship with drink over the next seventeen years or so grew out of that first night. I never liked the taste of alcohol in any form, but knew that, with enough of it inside me, I could be someone else, someone sharper, more confident, cleverer. It gave me the inner power to act the part of John Waters which I had written in my fantasies.

Without drink, I was incapable of functioning in ways that other people seemed to be able to function on the basis of personality alone. Drink became my substitute for a personality. With a couple of pints inside me, I could pass for normal.

Just as the world of Harry Potter breaks down into wizards and Muggles, so it seems to me now that the real world breaks down into those who by consent describe themselves as 'alcoholics' and people who can take a couple of drinks and leave it at that. The word 'alcoholic' is completely misunderstood by the Muggle world, so much so that I would never publicly use the word to describe myself. In the outside world, an alcoholic is someone lying in a gutter clutching a bottle of wine wrapped in a newspaper. He (it is stereotypically a 'he') has drunk the farm, beaten the wife and thrown away everything he ever had because of a craving for this liquid poison. It was never like that for me. Long after I stopped drinking, it was a shock for almost everyone who knew me that I had a problem with it in the first place. 'You were never like that,' they would say, meaning the tramp in the gutter with the brown bottle. It didn't matter. My problem with alcohol related to the extent to which I was incapable of functioning without it. How much or how often I drank didn't matter. In fact, I could give up drink for weeks, even months on end, but it took me many years to perceive that these breaks, far from signalling an absence of dependency, were themselves entirely focused on the occasion of the next drink, projected weeks or months into the future – my birthday, St Patrick's Day, the beginning of summer.

My problem derived from the fact that I needed alcohol in order to be even a shadow of a sociable human being. On the surface I was simply a young man who had perhaps become over-exuberant in his indulgence in the bottle. I hadn't drunk the farm, beaten the wife, or damaged my health beyond redemption. But when I reviewed my drinking years after they had ended, I became convinced that everything about me that worked at all had been built on a foundation of alcohol. I could mix with people, talk to women, dance with abandon, provided I had enough alcohol in my system to overcome whatever was preventing me from being normal without it.

The word 'alcoholic' is misleading as to the nature of the problem. It implies that the issue is a craving for this liquid which cannot be met in any other way. Certainly this is what it becomes in the later stages of a drinking decline. But that is not the essential nature of it. In the beginning the condition is defined by a need for something that makes you normal, if not exactly complete. One of the things I began to learn about after I stopped drinking was the ubiquitousness of fear in my life. Without knowing it, I had been afraid of everything: meeting people, conversation, waking up in the morning, going to sleep at night, telephones, unopened envelopes with my name on them, work, responsibility, police officers, people with English accents, fluent Irish speakers, people older than myself, people younger than myself, people my own age. I was afraid of big things and small things. I was afraid in the macro sense of fearing life and death and everything in between, and in the micro sense of not wanting to ask for directions in case my thick-tongued mumble led me into disgrace.

Drink cured all that, or, to be absolutely precise, I was relieved from all this fear when I had taken drink. Not only was I able to face people and situations that otherwise terrified me, but all the dead weight of accumulated little fears became dissipated by the second drink. Of course, all the things and situations that terrified me remained unaltered by my drinking (except when, sometimes, they were made much worse), but this perhaps said more about the nature of my fear than about the limitations of my drug of choice. Alcohol often gets a bad press, but it is important to record how effective it can be in meeting the needs of those who use or abuse it.

Modern society, with its pervasive hyper-rationality and supposedly limitless range of technological solutions to its publicly visible problems, has caused us to forget how relatively powerless the individual is to deal with issues for which society at large feels it has all the answers. In the past, such feelings of impotence were offset by a belief in God. One result of God's obliteration is that, without anyone, least of all the unbelieving individual, being especially conscious of this, human beings have been burdened with bellyfuls of fear, anxiety and sadness concerning things our antecedents regarded as the will and the responsibility of God. And, blinded to the true source of the problem, we seek increasingly ineffective and even more damaging palliatives for these feelings – drugs and alcohol having become the most readily available non-spiritual antidotes.

We live in a world which claims it has all the answers, but, as isolated, atomized human beings, we are secretly and deeply sceptical about rationality. Sitting in front of my computer screen, I feel at once in control of the universe and also terrified that, in truth, the scope of my extended reach through technology has made me more vulnerable rather than less. If, as sometimes occurs for no apparent reason, my computer behaves in a way that I have never seen it behave before, I find myself experiencing a fear that seems, on the face of it, to be utterly disproportionate to the situation. I may have inadvertently pressed some button or engaged some process which has altered the configuration of the text, or made visible the system of symbols reflecting the underlying organization system of the program I am using. I don't know how to get things back to normal. For a time, I become convinced that this is the worst thing that has ever happened in my life. I may go to bed for a night or two believing, in all seriousness, that my life will never be the same. Deeper down, I am aware of perceiving that, in some vague way, I have expected this to happen, that it is an event perfectly in tune with my innermost expectations. In this deeper sense of things, I am aware that my sense of technological adventuring has been an illusion, that I am now more helpless than if I had never owned a computer, and that this sudden remembrance does not really come as a surprise. It is often remarked that, the more ostensibly rational our culture becomes, the more the individual is cast back into superstition, because the poverty of religious thought has made us less, rather than more, rational. We are, in fact, in our very natures, profoundly sceptical about rationality, which means that, the greater our dependencies on things we do not understand or fully control (i.e. almost every aspect of our modern existence), the greater our secret need to admit our limits to ourselves and to life.

When I was drinking, I was oblivious of all this. I imagined that I was simply 'enjoying myself'. Of course, in a sense I was enjoying myself, but largely by virtue of the unconscious relief that the balm of alcohol brought me. If you had suggested to me that my life was governed by fear, I would have declared you mad, though I would probably have needed to get a couple of drinks in me beforehand.

And the fear was not just of the kind that can in retrospect be recognized and named. All kinds of rivulets of terror secreted themselves in the fabric of the everyday and would have rendered me immobile without the aid of alcohol. One of the things I began to see clearly after I stopped drinking was that the entire motivational mechanism of my working life was constructed around drink. I had placed drinking sessions strategically between bouts of work in such a way as to get me through what would otherwise have been an ordeal. When I stopped, I became immobilized for a while and had to reconstruct my system of self-motivation from the ground up. One of the reasons for this was that, when certain kinds of personalities are introduced to alcohol, they cease to develop for as long as the power of alcohol remains available to them. There is no need to learn emotional or other coping skills if all you have to do is fork out for a pint of beer. As a result, elements of the heavy drinker's psychological and emotional apparatus begin to atrophy. Without drink, he is like a bulb without power: inert, purposeless, waiting. With drink he is effervescent, exultant, alight.

In all Western societies, technology, fear of crime and a tyranny of choice are eroding people's quality of life, despite considerable material gains. Although we enjoy greater affluence, more advanced healthcare, a safer environment and a wider array of labour-saving gadgets than ever, a range of anxieties is hampering the growth of true contentment. Huge gains in material wealth have not accrued any significant increase in happiness. What we gain at one end of the equation we more than lose at the other. In Britain the proportion of people suffering from 'anxiety, depression or bad nerves' has almost doubled from just over 5 per cent in the past decade. About eight in ten people believe that Britain has become a more dangerous place over the same period. Ireland generally shows up in such research as more optimistic than Britain, but this may be because we are still benefiting from the residue of traditional society while relishing the novelty of the modern era.

We worry about big things and small, real and improbable. We worry about our children. Are they safe? Will they succeed in life? We worry about our jobs. Will we keep them? Will the multinational for which we work relocate to the Czech Republic?

Much of the anxiety affecting modern societies is covert and often banal. The rise of individualism and increasing specialization in the workplace means that few people have a full understanding of where they fit into the general picture, or of what their colleagues are doing: each function is discrete and self-justifying, leaving workers with the feeling that they are not important and could easily be dispensed with. For many, the blurring of boundaries between traditional male/female roles is leading to confusion, while for others the challenge of organizing leisure time with so much on offer is another unexpected source of stress. At the domestic level, a fear of science manifests itself in problems understanding the latest technology. 'Feature overload', whereby new gadgets are designed with so many extras that they are rendered almost impossible to use, means that, as one survey indicated, more than half of British people are unable to operate all the features of their video recorders, while nearly three-quarters are unable to use all the features of their personal computer. Nearly a third are baffled by microwave ovens. Mundane phenomena such as utility bills and pensions come with labyrinthine charging structures that can make them almost impossible to analyse. Some companies engage in what is actually called 'confusion marketing', deliberately seeking to hoodwink consumers. Every conceivable facet of human interchange and culture is nowadays broken down into market transactions, and the complexity of this process both boggles the mind of the individual and also multiplies the anxiety about some future collapse of earning potential, with technological complexity mirroring this confusion. We have obliterated many of the extraneous comforts which membership of human society used to confer – neighbourliness, courtesy, chivalry, and so forth – and replaced them with services which are available, sometimes with a smile and a 'Have a nice day', but which are deeply unsatisfactory by comparison with the encultured values that have been destroyed. This renders us utterly dependent on technological means to cope with even our most intimate needs or concerns, and also terrified that our ability to live in any kind of dignity, safety and comfort depends exclusively on our wealth/earning potential.

Here it becomes pertinent to consider the assassination of God that occurred in post-sixties culture in many Westernized societies. Previously, God acted as a kind of buffer between the human being and absolute responsibility to be in control of every aspect of his or her own life. Problems could be offered up, handed over or placed for mediation with the Blessed Virgin or Saint Anthony. Now, unless I am able to guarantee my own and my family's safety, security, comfort and happiness, the responsibility rests on my shoulders alone, and this causes me such intolerable anxiety and fear that I am unable to do even the most ordinary things without incurring further stress.

In all the debate about God, we seem to have missed the possibility that there is something in the human being that actually requires us to believe in an external power, an absolute horizon of responsibility, and that, without this mechanism, we are being shrivelled up with the fear that comes from having God's responsibilities without God's power. Fear has become the most pervasive element in the life of the modern citizen. Many of these fears remain not only invisible but also unacknowledged and, to a large extent, unconscious. Fear is the root source of addictive behaviours, and fear is really the absence of faith.

The 'rational' arguments about the non-existence of God impressed me for quite a while. I had strong motivations for taking them seriously. I wanted to be free. I wanted to be clever. I wanted to convince myself, not merely that I no longer needed to kowtow to those hypocritical priests and bishops, but that my life would become better, more honest, without these childish superstitions. I wanted to think of myself as a rational, reasonable, modern-minded human being.

There is little in the current frenzy of neo-atheistic material about God and his alleged non-existence that I did not at one time or another ventilate in my own life. Religion, because it fed tribalistic animus, was not merely foolish, but actively dangerous. Belief in God was an evolutionary fluke, a by-product of some once-useful cognitive function, a neurological accident. Religion was a hangover from the primitive mind, and the simple-mindedness of Irish Catholicism was the living proof of this.

Some of those who have set their caps against belief invariably consider that, in discussing the subject in the presence of believers, they are dealing with an intellectually inferior species. For many years I thought like that. It was self-evident, was it not, that anyone who believed that a dead body could rise again, or that water could be changed into wine, was suffering from delusions? It seemed to me that, required to choose between what was visible, intuitive and concrete and what was clearly counter-intuitive, immaterial and intangible, a rational person would choose the former. And, from the seemingly solid ground of this resolve, it appeared to follow that the phenomenon of belief had evolved from primitive limits to human understanding. Whatever man did not understand, he 'explained' as the actions of 'the gods'. In this, there was an implicit acceptance of the superiority of these gods and, by extension, of one's own inferiority. This did not appeal to me in the least. Religion was childish and old-fashioned. Moreover, I did not need it and could be freer without it.

I have come to a different point of view, and strangely do not now regard this view as less rational than the one I held before. I have come to this view through necessity. The neo-atheists would say that I have come to this position illogically. It appears to me obvious now that humans do not, cannot, know everything. Whereas many scientists tend to speak as if the present condition of relative unknow-ingness is a temporary and receding condition, my own sense is that the unknowability of reality is of an infinite nature. Faced with infinity and eternity, my most reasonable response is to admit my limitations. One of the ways in which I trace my steps for a partial explanation of my belief is to say that I had, to begin with, a need. After two decades of believing myself to be the master of myself and, to an extent, of my destiny, I came to realize that I was at sea in the universe. Eventually, I came back to the idea of God as something useful to me, something necessary for my correct alignment in the world. Didn't George Bernard Shaw once say something to the effect that the human mind is such a complex and intricate instrument that it surpasses its own ability to comprehend itself? Maybe the difference between what we understand and what we don't understand we choose to call God. Or maybe all the 'rationalizations' and 'explanations' as to why God does not exist are themselves dissolved by the possibility that an omni-potent, all-seeing God must surely have anticipated them. Put another way, isn't it likely that God, if He exists at all, created us in such a way as to make human belief in him a natural, if not instinctive, phenomenon? Establishing, therefore, that 'religious' belief is some-thing we seem to have created in our own heads becomes tautologous.

Arriving at a scientific explanation for why our brains seek to imagine deities may, therefore, amount to no more than a clearer understanding of the way God works within us.

None of this, of course, confirmed God's existence, but it did enable me to re-establish solidarity with those who have continued to believe in Him. I began to see that such people were not necessarily irrational, still less stupid. They were behaving in accordance with the rational configuration of their need. Believing in God is a choice I make based on my need and on my nature. I don't really know if God exists or not, but I have long believed that, even if He doesn't, we humans have an urgent necessity to imagine Him.

There remains in modern society the perception that drug and alcohol abuse is some kind of isolated siding into which people get shunted for various reasons to do with their exposure to drink and/or drugs. This may be partly true, but it is probably also the case that, if an individual who becomes addicted had not taken up alcohol, he or she would very likely have fallen into some other kind of self-destructive behaviour, and this, rather than the particular crutch that is chosen, is what needs to be observed. There is, in other words, an underlying condition which renders an individual susceptible to addiction. I also happen to believe that, while this may have certain symptoms which exist within the individual, there is also a societal dimension.

More than six decades ago, William D. Silkworth, a medical doctor consulted by the embryonic Alcoholics Anonymous, defined two of the key symptoms of alcoholism as physical allergy and mental compulsion. This means that (a) the body of an alcoholic is not the same as the body of a non-alcoholic; and (b) those who drink abusively are drinking to overcome a craving beyond their mental control. The only hope of recovery, Dr Silkworth asserted, is 'an entire psychic change'.

It is an article of faith in Alcoholics Anonymous that alcoholism is a disease. And this disease, according to Silkworth's analysis, can be cured only by a spiritual transformation. Up to a point I am comfortable enough with the idea that what we know as alcoholism, like many forms of addiction, is some kind of spiritual malaise, though I have problems with the way this concept can be employed by some alcoholics to absolve themselves responsibility for their actions. If their condition is a 'disease', they reckon, they can't be blamed when it breaks out every so often like a recurring rash. This, I believe, is dangerous foolishness. But, such is the paradoxical nature of this condition that I also recognize the lack of usefulness in deconstructing the disease theory. This is a classic example of a topic in which the 'truth' may not be as useful as a certain form of constructed, workable error. Anyone who ever managed to overcome a problem with alcohol has lots of theories about what alcoholism is, but most of these theories remain largely untested because none of them is worth the risk of it being wrong.

I gave up drinking at the age of 35. Everyone who drinks even a little too much has a satchelful of colourful anecdotes of atrocities, calamities, near misses, and excruciating episodes of what amounts to a public breakdown of personal identity owing to intoxication or alcoholic decline. The incidents of themselves are not important. What matters is that I once drank a fair deal, couldn't handle it and stopped. When people ask me nowadays why I don't drink, I respond with a line from the comedian Billy Connolly, 'I wanted to stop while it was still my own idea.' It conveys the reality to those clued-in enough to hear, dissipates the tension that seems to gather around such discussions in Ireland, and saves time.

I had briefly encountered Alcoholics Anonymous a couple of years before, when I went to meetings for a few months, but had broken out later and, while understanding my own need to be rid of the bottle, did not feel motivated enough to go back. I therefore spent five years as what I later heard described as a 'dry drunk'; that is, someone who gives up alcohol without a spiritual programme. It worked for me, in the sense that I managed to stay away from alcohol. Later on, events occurred in my life which, though ostensibly unconnected to drinking, brought me to a point where I recalled the warmth I had encountered on first entering the rooms of AA, and, having no other options, decided to see what it might offer. Over the next few years I was able to obtain a sense of the topography of my condition which revolutionized my thinking about myself.

Soon, for example, I gained insight into why the fellowship of AA looks askance at the idea of trying to give up drink on the basis of willpower alone. The programme of AA insists that willpower is not enough, and the 'Big Book' refers to alcohol as 'cunning, baffling, powerful'.

Because there are different levels of intensity associated with various compulsive/addictive behaviours, some are relatively easy to treat and others almost impossible. Some such behaviours may well be resolved by willpower alone. Others require a rewriting of the mental programme which, by creating and maintaining certain associations, serves to propel the addictive behaviour. Invariably, these programmes have to do with either pleasurable or painful associations concerning the addictive behaviour, and it is necessary to deconstruct these logics if the addictive behaviour is to be overcome.

Willpower can work with less virulent addictions, such as cigarette smoking (cigarette addicts will not agree). But there are some addictions which, by their nature, have an inbuilt defence against almost any attempt to rewrite the underlying belief system, and an addiction to alcohol is one such. The issue is not whether or not the condition is genetic, or even if it has, for example, an allergenic dimension – the point is that it occurs beyond the normal reach of the individual's ability to self-correct. Because alcohol is a mood-altering drug, it sabotages attempts to rearrange the belief system that has created the addiction. In AA they say that alcoholism is the only disease that constantly tells you that you don't have it. But more fundamentally, the very nature of the inebriated state, or indeed the mindset which persistent drunkenness engenders, is utterly resistant to attempts to constructively change the personality of the sufferer. The state of inebriation is so attractive, and the escape so complete while it lasts, that, without some additional elements being brought to bear, the alcoholic mindset rejects even the notion that change is necessary. It resists intervention in the way a drowning man fights off his rescuer.

The outside world anticipates Alcoholics Anonymous as a fanatical cult which brainwashes its members against the evils of indulgence. No, AA offers perhaps the most sensational programme for living that has ever been presented in one coherent entity and suggests, yes suggests, that, if you want to begin living a decent and happy life, you think about following it. The programme of AA amounts to a distillation of the wisdom of the ages, gathered together by desperate but brilliant minds, as an arsenal against the encroachment of the dark side of human nature. It calls itself a 'spiritual programme' and certainly it offers a spiritual prescription. But it is first and foremost a psychological programme, which, knowing the nature of the mentality it is dealing with, presents a staged and digestible blueprint for dealing with life's difficulties.

The 'one day at a time' concept is a classic example of something that is known about on the outside but utterly misunderstood. In the logic of the Muggle world, one day at a time conveys a clinging onto sobriety in spite of near overwhelming temptation, a joyless existence filled with dreams about drink. But although embracing the idea of not drinking for today, the concept is not primarily related to drink at all. What it tells me is that today is both the only day I have to endure and also the only day that is available to me. I should not, therefore, either allow it to overwhelm me or allow it to slip away untasted. On any given day, either one of these imperatives will be uppermost. I have had days filled with fear, when the total implications of an unfolding situation caused me to become paralysed with terror, and have found myself able to unravel that terror by remembering that I need to survive only until bedtime. Sufficient unto the day is the evil thereof. On other days, I have found myself so focused on some future event – a date, my birthday, seeing my beloved daughter again – that I have been absent from the present moment. The programme tells me to live now, right where I am. It tells me to smell the flowers as I walk along and to wear my best shirt today.

The literature of Alcoholics Anonymous is very specific about the physiological dimension of the condition. Alcoholism, it insists, is a 'disease'. My belief is that this notion, if taken too literally, can be unhelpful to the alcoholic in need of a good shoe up the backside. But in general, again, it works. And the reason it works, I believe, is this: in order to impress upon the still suffering addict that his own sense of powerlessness is not the definitive word on the subject, it is necessary to allow him off the hook of absolute responsibility for his condition. This both reassures him in relation to various previous failed attempts at giving up the booze, and also prepares him for the central plank of the AA programme: the idea of God As We Understand Him.

I have never met anyone who had a problem with alcohol who could say that they had been cured to the extent of becoming a normal social drinker again. There are, of course, people who stop drinking without the help of AA, but there is a complete absence of information as to how they are faring in the contexts that AA's philosophy has identified as central to the total rehabilitation of the addict. And, of course, those alcoholics who go back to drinking invariably provide poor evidential back-up for those who say there are ways of curing alcoholism outside of total abstinence in AA. It may well be that its principles work in a sense that is mistaken or misleading, but the danger of too much deconstruction is obvious. In a context where most of those requiring treatment come in at their lowest ebb – physically, mentally and spiritually – it is necessary for the programme to explain itself in the simplest terms possible. There is in AA an ingrained opposition to analysis of its principles – they talk of 'paralysis by analysis' – purely because any sense of the paradoxical nature, complexity or ambiguity of some of the principles might not be helpful to the addict just in off the street. In this context, the disease theory does a job. Call it a necessary simple-mindedness

Alcoholics Anonymous sets out to achieve two things: to reconstruct the mindset of the alcoholic and to restore the fractured relationship of the alcoholic with God. Generally speaking, these two objectives amount to the same thing. But before that, and as an absolute prerequisite, the sufferer has to be persuaded that he is not, himself, God. There is a book which one occasionally encounters in AA called *Not-God: A History of Alcoholics Anonymous*, in which the author, Ernest Kurtz, reminds his readers that 'the fundamental and first message of Alcoholics Anonymous to its members is that they are not infinite, not absolute, not God. Every alcoholic's problem had first been, according to this insight, claiming God-like powers, especially that of control.' Kurtz's book is a dense but a richly rewarding work for anyone seeking a deeper understanding of addiction in its social context. He identifies alcoholism as a disease, rather a 'dis-ease', of modernity, an expression of the human being's confusion at the fracturing of the human personality, the separation of the physical from the mental from the spiritual in a rational, secular, industrial context. Centrally, AA seeks to lead the recovering alcoholic to a reintegration of these three elements, defining alcoholism as a threefold – 'physical, mental, spiritual' – disease. In his scintillating analysis of addiction as a by-product of modernity, Kurtz quotes my middle-namesake Saint Augustine: 'Our hearts are restless until they rest in Thee.' At the back of AA's 'spiritual programme', writes Kurtz, is the idea that it is precisely 'this thirst for transcendence that expressed itself in the alcoholic's addictive, obsessive-compulsive drinking. The thirst for transcendence had been perverted into a thirst for alcohol . . . [One of AA's founders] Bill Wilson at times observed to trusted correspondents that the alcoholic seemed to be an especially sensitive person, one haunted by a particularly pressing need for transcendence. That, he and others suggested, was why the spiritual programme of Alcoholics Anonymous worked. It spoke to the need for transcendence by offering the alcoholic real contact with the spiritual.' Addiction is prone to strike free spirits who have glimpsed Infinity while remaining imprisoned in their earthly bodies. The alcoholic, having dreamt of transcendence, cannot abide 'real' life, but desires to be in heaven, right here, right now, all the time.

It is possible to be around AA and have a profound sense of the spiritual dimension of the programme, a sense replicating that of one's early childhood about God and goodness and so forth. It is also possible to survive in AA and have a sense that the ingenious AA concept of 'God As I Understand Him' is simply a clever psychological trick, designed to lure the addict out of his own dualistic sense of omnipotence/impotence, and into a more relaxed, surrendering frame of mind. In other words, God in AA terms may be more a psychological than a spiritual phenomenon. It is possible, indeed, for a recovering alcoholic to remain unconvinced about God and still gain the benefit of having a functioning Higher Power in his life. The point is that sincerity doesn't matter: willingness is all. This approach has been found to work, possibly because, in Western societies, almost everyone grows up with some sense of a God, and has therefore a hardwired association between God and goodness, morality, virtue, restraint and all the other values which we tend to associate with the religious part of our upbringing. Thus, AA reconditions the rusty mechanism which once drove the individual alcoholic's sense of moral rectitude. In doing so, it restores the remembered moral framework of the individual, but it also does something else: it relieves the individual of the burden of worrying about the world, of carrying the weight of every detail of existence on a single pair of frail shoulders.

A central element of the AA programme is the idea that people who have abused alcohol have done so because they are seeking to fill a 'God-shaped hole' in their psyches. But there is also an apparently paradoxical tendency to seek to occupy the throne God has been forced to vacate, and this is telling in respect of the wider experience of a society which has abandoned its faith, in which addictions of numerous kinds are multiplying. The fundamental problem has been that drugs and alcohol enable the addict to feel, falsely and temporarily, that his becoming God may not be such a preposterous idea after all. By dulling his sense of personal impotence, his drug of 'choice' lulls him into a feeling of omnipotence, which remains for as long as the drug is functional and available.

In the AA and drug rehab. recovery programmes, therefore, God is, in this sense, purely functional as a way of counteracting the previous functionality of alcohol. Really, what the AA blueprint does is to set about rewriting the mental programmes of addicts, using their own idea of God as the ultimate witness, since experience has shown that this offers the best chance of getting the rewritten programme to take. This same process also replaces the chemical dependency, born of fear and a sense of inadequacy, with precisely that which it displaced in the course of its virulent assault. There is a chapter in the 'Big Book' (formerly known as Alcoholics Anonymous), entitled 'We Agnostics', which in its deadpan title conveys the reality of alcoholism: all alcoholics, whether it appears to be so or not, have succumbed to the temptation to remove God from His throne and take the seat themselves.

Those who graduate through Alcoholics Anonymous are warned of, among many things, the dangers of complacency, of describing yourself as cured. The programme of AA does not promise to turn you into someone who no longer drinks, but only to help the alcoholic to resist the first drink, one day at a time. By AA logic, I will never be 'cured' of alcoholism but am sober today by the grace of God. I understand the logic of this, but no longer feel bound by it. I think of myself nowadays as an ex-drinker. I don't believe I will ever drink again. This doesn't mean I am complacent, but it does mean that I no longer see myself as someone who has to spend every waking moment on guard against the revisitation of addiction.

Another thing that is discouraged in AA is the idea of people who have come through the fellowship making public statements about the programme, such as I'm doing by writing about my experience here. There is a good reason for this also: if someone who has declared publicly that they have come through the programme were to relapse, this might discourage others from seeking the help they need, on the basis that the programme doesn't seem to work. Again, there is an irrefutable logic in this, but it seems to me that the world today, perhaps more than ever, has a need to hear about how AA has managed to save millions of people from a grisly and ignominious demise. Alcoholism is itself already a death of the spirit, but untreated it has but two outcomes: madness and literal, physical death.

# — 5 —

# Desperate Dan

The moment I began to understand what prayer was could hardly have been less holy, at least in the conventional sense. As a pious child I would have retreated from it, horrified. Even now I find myself torn between revulsion and a kind of wonder.

I was sitting in a room, listening to a man talking about his daily prayers. It was a large room, filled in that southside Dublin lunchtime with an assortment of human beings, the majority of whom were men. They were listening attentively to the speaker, a man in his early fifties.

The speaker was at pains to make clear that he did not believe in God. Let us call him 'Pete'. He was talking about 'the God thing'. His story in this respect was not unlike mine. He had been, or imagined he had been, an intense believer as a child, but had turned away in adulthood to pursue a more earthly flight path. He too had taken to drink as a way of camouflaging his social awkwardness. He related a litany of atrocities much more spectacular than mine. And then he got to the point of transformation, his encountering of Alcoholics Anonymous and, broken beyond rebellion, his embrace of its programme for sobriety.

The God Bit, he said had always caused him difficulty. He wanted to believe, but couldn't. Believing would have made his life simple, but his scepticism was too great. He was a film-maker, clearly well read and widely travelled. He talked about the values of the sixties revolution, his love of rock 'n' roll, his sense that God was part of the establishment. He had been brought up in the Catholic Church but had rejected it outright. He couldn't see himself ever going back. At this point I may have yawned at the familiarity of the story.

And yet, he said, he prayed every day.

I watched and listened to him carefully from the moment he said this. He was older than I then was, perhaps by a decade or so. His hair was short, but had the appearance of having been shorn under something of a protest. There are men who look comfortable with short hair and men who, no matter how they try to disguise it, communicate a wildness of spirit from underneath the severest of GI haircuts. He had a full head of hair which betrayed a hint of chestnut dye. There were bits sticking out, as though in a hurry to grow again. He wore a leather jacket and had a pair of shades hanging from the v of his open-necked shirt. I fancied I recognized him as a near stereotypical child of the flower-power generation, and this was pretty much the gist of his self-description. But then he described himself getting down on his knees every morning and every night. This is what he had been told to do, he said, in spite of his unbelief. In order to overcome his alcoholism, he elaborated, 'they' had told him that he had to hand his will and his life over to a Power greater than Pete. He hadn't accepted this, still less understood it – in fact, he had rejected it with every bone in his body. How could he hand his will and his life over to someone or something that didn't exist? Because, they said, he had no choice: alcohol had beaten him, and, for as long as he remained alone and isolated, it would return, perhaps eventually to kill him. 'They' told him that he could choose anything that suited him to represent the Higher Power. He could choose the group to which he belonged and to which he was now speaking. He could choose his dead father. He could choose the light bulb dangling over his head. But, if he was ever to achieve peace from the demons in his soul, he would have to find something onto which to unburden some of the responsibility for his daily existence. 'They' talked to him about their understanding of God, which they called 'God as we understand Him'. The trouble was, said Pete, that he didn't hardly understand God at all, and the bits he did understand he regarded with fear and loathing. Then, one of 'them' had suggested: 'Fake it till you make it': pretend that you believe in God, act as if you do, and note what happens. Think of yourself as a child again, helpless before reality, and go through the motions of asking for divine help. 'And this might work?' he had asked them incredulously. 'Yes', they said, 'it will work well enough to get you to the next stage.' And what, he wondered, was 'the next stage'? 'Believing,' they said. 'And after that?' 'Calling what you believe in "God",' they explained.

He had found this wildly implausible but still he had done as they said. Except that he had never quite made it to the next stage. He was stuck, he thought, halfway between unbelief and belief. He prayed every morning and every night to a God he didn't believe in. He found it useful but couldn't overcome what he called his 'rational' impulse.

Then he proposed that he would share with the group the nature of this paradoxical prayer. He paused as though waiting for acquiescence, a moment of something that might have been taken for reverence. 'God,' Pete's prayer began, 'you bollox.' The room went pale. 'If you exist, which you clearly don't, get your finger out and give me a dig-out today. Amen.'

Several people in the room laughed raucously, others giggled nervously, and not a few looked horrified or disgusted. I was shocked, less by what Pete had said than by his willingness to say it out like that in front of a mixed group of people. I didn't know how I should react. Laughter didn't seem the right response, not because what he had said was verging on the sacrilegious, but because I gathered from his demeanour that he was trying to get to something beyond humour or sensation.

Then Pete told how, although sceptical to begin with, he had found these 'prayers' to be effective. He didn't quite know how, or even if, there was a direct connection, but from about the time he started to get down on his knees twice a day and utter this, to my ears, blasphemous ejaculation, his life had got better. Even as I was thinking that Pete had uttered a blasphemy, I was aware of the intrinsic ludicrousness of the thought: how can you blaspheme against a God who doesn't exist? But perhaps it struck me – I don't recall now – that this was no more intrinsically ludicrous than the idea of being helped by the same non-existent God he didn't believe in. I was also taken by the fact that, although Pete was doing something that contradicted his 'rational' impulse and had found it to work, his 'rational' impulse had remained, at a conscious level at least, resistant to the idea that what was happening might, by virtue of its success, have the right to a 'rational' status of its own.

Pete went on to outline in detail the complex mechanism by which he initially managed to get himself onto his knees. This had been an important part of it, he said. Every fibre of his being, he recalled, had at first resisted the idea. His very limbs revolted at assuming a posture which implied, for him, subservience, weakness and domination. His knees would not bend for prayer. But 'they' had an answer for this as well: he should throw one of his shoes under the bed so he had to get on his knees to retrieve it, and while he was down there he should say a prayer or two. I laughed out loud at this, but thought it strange that nobody else did. Later I came to realize that this was because it was a line that the rest of the group would have heard many times before.

I listened to Pete as he went on to emphasize that he still didn't believe. He had found that what 'they' had told him was true: his life had begun to get better and it seemed, as though by what he would have regarded as coincidence, to have started to change from the time he began to pray in this outrageous manner. His life became more manageable. The compulsion to drink disappeared. He was happier than he had been for a long time. But still he could not overcome many years of prejudice and scepticism. Moreover the piety of religion scared the life out of him. If there was a God, which he again emphasized there wasn't, he fancied such a Being would be able to tolerate a little jocular abuse. Maybe, he concluded, one day he would arrive at the pearly gates to discover that the God of his childhood actually existed, and was just as humourless and power-hungry as he had been led to believe. But he would continue to take his chances. It didn't worry him all that much.

When people ask me if I am religious, I almost always say 'No'. I anticipate what I think they mean by that and decide either that saying 'Yes' will give them a false impression, if not altogether close down their sense of who I am, or that, in the sense that they mean anyway, I am not religious at all. These options appear to amount to the same thing, but they don't quite. In one case I am anticipating prejudice; in the other misunderstanding.

If someone asks me if I believe in God, it becomes a little simpler, though not much. I always say 'Yes' to this question, but generally tend to be less definite when answering an Irish person, even, perhaps especially, a Catholic cleric. With foreigners including Catholic foreigners, I say 'Yes' and then go on to explain the precise nature of my belief. With Irish people I am more circumspect. If the questioner is someone I recognize as a 'traditional' Irish Catholic, I may equivocate a little for fear of implying a fellow feeling that, in truth, fills me with a subtle form of unease. It is nothing personal, just the accumulated effect of several decades of conditioning and reaction. If I am talking to an Irish secularist, atheist or agnostic, I may pronounce the 'Yes' with more certainty, but only for bravado. The only people I am completely happy discussing God with are other members of AA or, latterly, members of Communion and Liberation, an odd and interesting Catholic organization founded in Italy in the 1950s by Father Luigi Giussani, which brought itself to my notice a couple of years ago and continues to intrigue me. With AA members, in particular, I find a common sense of the purpose and meaning of words. In AA, it doesn't matter if someone remains an atheist or agnostic, which, in spite of everything, many members of the fellowship do. There are so many multiple levels of understanding in AA as to the meanings of words such as 'God', 'spirit', 'faith' and 'morality' that conversations between alcoholics tend to be looser, less prescriptive than conversations in the outside world. AA members may not agree about the final meaning of things, but they have a guaranteed mutuality of understanding in respect of both the context and purpose of the language associated with God.

My faith, such as it is, is new and raw. It is not something I can loudly proclaim, because it is fragile, tentative and full of doubt. It is not a faith I have received from anyone or anywhere but one forged in the white heat of my own experience. It is mine alone, like my nose.

If faith depended on holiness, I would be damned. The idea that I have a faith or a religious dimension has no obvious implications for my personality, at least not in any of the ways that it would be expected to have in the conventional understandings of what is, to a large extent, a post-Catholic Ireland. I swear, try to evade paying at parking meters and look around in the street at beautiful women as much as I ever did, possibly more.

Concepts such as that one 'believes', 'is a believer', has 'the faith', has 'returned to the faith', 'goes to mass' and other related notions, all have graduated meanings in the culture of modern Ireland. Each is pregnant with meaning and, upon delivery in respect of an individual, immediately begins the writing of a cultural profile which hardens like concrete and can be revised with the greatest of difficulty. People who believe but want to avoid this, tend to use evasive phraseology, such as 'I'm a spiritual person', which means nothing and everything, and, because it has acquired such common usage, is rapidly becoming just as limiting as any of the old terminologies.

What I am, religiously speaking, is not just difficult to pin down – it is positively dangerous to articulate. I believe in God, though not necessarily all the time. It's not that I any longer have the immediate necessity to believe in order to save me from the lash of alcohol, but that my experiences in that regard have alerted me to something I previously had no insight into. My belief is therefore a choice I make, indeed remake all the time, rather than something I have been told is right or good for me, though one of my few certainties in this regard is that it is overwhelmingly a good thing. I don't know what this God of mine looks like, though sometimes I realize that, at the back of my mind, I still have an image of an old man with a bald crown and long white hair. I don't worry about the patent absurdity of this, because I know my mind needs stuff to build with. I'm also reminded of the belief in AA that a return journey from agnosticism will almost inevitably take you back to where you started, to the faith of your childhood.

A strange thing: after I began to edge my way back to belief, it was with God the Father that I found the greatest ease. One of the amazing pieces of advice handed around in AA, for example, is that when you have to face an ordeal of some kind – for example a court case or a job interview – you should pause at the door before entering the dreaded building or room, and stand back momentarily to invite God as You Understand Him to enter the room before you. I know how ridiculous it sounds. The reason alcoholics have found themselves able to try these bizarre strategies is because they have arrived at a place where, knowing what it is like to have nothing much to lose, they find themselves regaining things they imagined they had lost for ever. Having clawed your way out of the gutter, opening the door for God seems like a small price to pay for the reurn of your life and dignity.

I have given a great deal of thought to the fact that, even yet, it is God the Father I see, rather than His Son. Even though, in theory, Jesus would seem like the perfect companion with whom to develop a fourth-dimensional relationship, I resisted Him for several years, perhaps because His very name is burdened with so much baggage that I'm not sure I can extricate him from the cultural left-luggage department. But there was, I am convinced, another reason. My father died in 1989, which was about halfway between my first tentative experiments with putting aside the bottle and my final decision to do so. I believe now that these events were connected. When my father was alive, my relationship with him remained that of father–son, man–boy. When he died, we became one. On his death, my father entered my imagination in a way he could never have done while alive. I began to understand him as a spirit at a much deeper level than I had as a man. Freed of the burden of earthly authority, he became available to me in the totality of my personality, my flaws and weakness, my stupidity and my lack of belief. When I first tried out the AA Higher Power thing, it was my father I connected with. This, and because I recalled that my father's most intense devotion while alive seemed to be to the Virgin Mary, is part of the reason why I did not begin to relate the resuscitation of my faith to Jesus Christ. I am only now beginning to encounter, as though for the first time, the utterly staggering dimensions of the earthly life story of Jesus, to grapple with the idea that, just once in history, God came among us to tell us that everything would be all right. I am only beginning to glimpse the possibility that this story may answer my most fundamental questions in the way nothing else has ever done.

I know almost nothing of theology, at least nothing structured or chronologically coherent. What I believe, most fundamentally, is that I know as much about God as anyone who has ever drawn breath. Why? Because I was born charged with the question whose answer juts deep into Mystery. Because I am part of this Mystery. Because I am awe-struck by the wonder of the world. Because I did not make a molecule of myself. Because I do not know anything, and the more I learn, the less I seem to understand, which is to say the more I advance into the Mystery. 'Only the hypothesis of God,' wrote Father Luigi Giussani in his brilliant book *The Religious Sense*, 'only the affirmation of the mystery as a reality existing beyond our capacity to fathom entirely, only this hypothesis corresponds to the human person's original structure. If it is human nature to indomitably search for an answer, if the structure of a human being is, then, this irresistible and inexhaustible question, plea – then one suppresses the question if one does not admit to the existence of an answer. But this answer cannot be anything but unfathomable. Only the existence of the mystery suits the structure of the human person, which is mendacity, insatiable begging, and what corresponds to him is neither he himself nor something he gives to himself, measures or possesses.' This, for me, was a startling concept: that the appetite for God was not only part of my essential structure as a human being, but that the elemental nature of this structure was that it could not be satisfied by anything other than God. My thirsting, therefore, had been an expression both of the insatiability of my human appetites when directed at earthly things, and of my deep need for this one thing that could quench it.

The Mystery informs my life and, without the Mystery, that life has no meaning. Even when I deny the Mystery, it impels me in spite of myself. All my longings are ultimately directed at this Mystery, and anything else I seek to settle these longings on will turn to dust. Nothing of earthly life should be allowed to settle, to form itself into an ultimate meaning, because this will kill both the thing in question and the spirit I invest in it. Only by acknowledging the unknowable can I remain alive – but not, as I was told, because it is my duty to pay homage to the God Who Made Me, but because the unknowable is where my home is, where I come from, and where I am returning. I am of the unknowable and, therefore, in denying God, deny myself.

From time to time I have found myself in the throes of some intense emotion and being baffled by both the enormity and the disproportionality of it. It might be disappointment over lost love, or sadness, or fear, but when I try to equate the dimensions of it with its object, there usually seems to be this mismatch of cause and effect. It is as though there is something missing, something behind the feeling that comes from somewhere else. I read in Father Giussani's wonderful book that sadness – for instance – is 'a spark which is generated by the lived "potential difference" (to use an electrical term) between the ideal destination and its historical unfulfillment'. To be aware of the value of such sadness is to be conscious 'of the greatness of life and to intuit life's destiny'.

I have come some distance on the trail of that destiny but am only really beginning a journey that will, I am certain, have no ending. The farther I advance, the more space I open up before me.

In the beginning, as Pete had advised, I faked it. I acted out the ritual of belief, getting down on my knees each morning and night, asking for help, summoning the presence of a Being I didn't believe in to help me in whatever way He felt appropriate. But I took careful note of the outcomes, which I found to be remarkably counter-intuitive.

For a start I found that my prayers were answered. One of the complaints I'd had about God when I was a child was that He never did what I asked of Him. This had contributed in no small part to my sense of religion as a meaningless husk, a miserable pretence that added the misery of solemnity to life's staple stock of hardship and calamity. But someone in AA suggested to me that my prayers should, ideally, limit themselves to one word: 'Help!' My childhood prayers had themselves carried the essence of my erroneous under-standing of God and my own burgeoning desire to take His place in my life. If I avoided being prescriptive, I was advised, God would respond with a solution that would defy my own modest capacities to untangle my problems. It seemed implausible but I tried it anyway. Time and again, it worked. Whenever I encountered an intractable problem or an insoluble fear, instead of working out the solution I wanted, and then asking God to support it, I would simply surrender and ask to be rescued. And rescued I would be.

Getting down on my knees seemed an important part of it. At the beginning, as I say, I resisted this with all my mind and heart. The idea of making myself subservient to any other being, even a Supreme Being, filled me with distaste. Why should I bow and scrape before the Almighty? Even if He did exist, why couldn't we just sit down together and have a man-to-man conversation? Perhaps from His point of view, we could do this, and perhaps for some people this is the way to do it. But in my experience, the act of getting to my knees was a profoundly important part of the process, which was fundamentally about me rather than the Being I was addressing.

I had been bringing to the occasion of my prayers a set of prejudices born of the onset of agnosticism, more than twenty years earlier, focusing on the idea of a surrender to a vain and capricious God who needed to have me bowing and scraping at His feet before he would condescend to help me. It was something I heard at an AA meeting that caused me to turn it around. A man was talking, again, about prayer, and how he achieved it. 'The only proper posture for a human being in relation to his God', he said, 'is on his knees.' It would have been easy to hear this in an old way. But something in his appearance or demeanour struck a chord of recognition. Again, he did not strike me as a Holy Joe. What he was seeking to articulate seemed to go deeper than the conventional pieties I had grown up with. I asked him about it after the meeting and he briefly regarded the intensity of my question with the amusement of recognition. 'Kneeling down isn't primarily about God,' he said. 'It's about you. You need to kneel in order to understand your relationship to reality.' It was a mind-blowing idea. I didn't need to hear any more but wanted to go home immediately and start trying it out – that the source of All Power in the universe could become available to me, but only if I began to acknowledge my own smallness. Woh! I began to pray with this in mind. That I was nothing, or almost nothing, and yet a part of Everything. That the meaning of my getting down on my knees had to do, not with a crude idea of adoration, but with dramatizing the nature of my relationship with Everything. That out of a willingness to acknowledge abject powerlessness might emerge a connection to the Source of All Power. It was the most sensational thing I had ever heard in my life, and I was certain that I was hearing it for the first time. After that I began to focus, not on my position, but on the process I was engaged in. There was something exhilarating about it, if only at first its novelty after two decades of refusal.

I was intoxicated by the idea that I could change myself in this fundamental way. But then it struck me that the most salient element of this change was that I was adopting a posture in which it was implicit that I was no longer the one in charge. The act of getting on my knees was symbolic of a new relationship with the world, in which I accepted my relative insignificance. I was abdicating from the throne I had stolen from God.

At first I did it reluctantly. I never had to descend to the recommended strategy of throwing a shoe under the bed, but there was, for a long time, a stiffness in my joints that did not come from any physical condition. But then things began to change. First I stopped worrying about the subservience suggested by my posture. 'So what?' I asked myself. Nobody could see me. Then I began to feel in my 'subservience' a sense of freedom.

At first I didn't really think about myself as adoring a Superior Being. I thought of myself as engaging in a dialogue with Something or Someone who could help me. The kneeling became, in the initial stages, simply a way of marking the occasion out from other activities. I knelt to pray in the same way that I sat down to have breakfast or lay down to sleep. It began to suggest itself as important for me to have this different posture, if only to distinguish the procedure and mark it as having at least as much significance as eating and sleeping. It was some time before I began to understand it in a different way, but eventually, as I had been told, I began to feel that the kneeling posture was less about God than about me.

From then it seemed as if the entire world had started to move in a different way. Solutions to seemingly intractable problems would come, not directly in terms of a solution to whatever problematic situation I found myself encountering but usually out of some extraordinary alteration. The difficulty would simply dissolve, sometimes leaving no logical explanation behind. I would pray as best I could, withholding all prescriptions; I would get on my knees and admit my inability to resolve my difficulties. I would recite stock prayers which I had learned by heart, prayers about acceptance and surrender, and would go to bed at night resolving that I had exhausted my personal capacities and had put myself at the mercy of something far, far greater than myself. Always, always, the circumstances would begin to change. It was as though, in prayer, I was prising myself through some chink into the fourth dimension, into an incrementally enhancing harmony with an invisible, infinite reality. But the invisibility of this reality did not in any way render it spooky or airy-fairy. Experience, time and time again, told me it was there. There appeared to be a logic to it, but not one that I could work out in my head, rather a logic that could be apprehended only by a process of feeling, of intuition. I could feel when it was working and when it was not. Always, too, its failure to work when it did not work had to do with me, with my inability to stop worrying about the problem with my limited consciousness. Sometimes I would be able to predict, not the precise outcome, but the general configuration of the solution. Some vague sense would arise out of my experience that everything was going to be all right. I would know from the way I felt in advance of the event I'd been in dread of that none of the things I feared would come true. And they would not. The scenes cloistered in the darkest recesses of my negativity would never be played out. Always things would change, sometimes suddenly and shockingly, other times subtly and slowly. After a time, it was as though my intellect had discovered a new form of rationalism, one based not on logic and what seemed plausible, but on the often impossible outcomes of my own experience.

Out of this I intuited several things. That Something undoubtedly existed which I did not understand, beyond luck or coincidence or superstition. That this Something was not far away, up in the sky, or in any other sense remote from my reality, but immersed in that reality, or perhaps immersing it. That this Something might be said to amount to another Reality, one sharing space with the one I was familiar with, but adhering to different rules. The logic that revealed itself from the workings of these rules and the behaviour of this different Reality made no sense in terms of the thought processes of the 'real' world. To try to explain it to someone who wished to remain unreceptive was a fool's errand. To observe it was to manifest two opposing responses even within oneself. One response was that this was utterly unbelievable, that the effects that appeared to emanate from the alleged alternative reality were in fact the consequence of coincidence and nothing more. The other was that this pattern of effects had about it a certain level of irrefutability. It was consistent and consistently logical on its own terms. It seemed to obey some amorphous principles which remained slightly out of the range of rational definition, but which seemed to define themselves nonetheless by virtue of the patterns they repeated. The results became, if not predictable, in a certain sense inevitable. It was possible to tell by the quality of the connection I felt at any particular time with this other Reality how certain and definitive would be the solution to whatever the problem happened to be.

The only requirements appeared to be that I asked for help and did whatever I felt was my duty and within my capability. A principle I heard often in AA rooms showed up to be tested: if I do God's work, He will do mine. The corollary of this, it was pointed out to me, was that I would have to do the things I was able to, and then stand out of God's way. This involved a process of calibration with regard to acquiring some kind of intuitive understanding as to where God's work began and where mine ended. It was not a perfect science. It was prone to error, to underachievement and excess of endeavour. The strange thing is that this hardly seemed to matter if the intention was right. I don't mean 'right' in some objective catechismal sense, but right in the sense that, at that precise moment, to the best of my ability, it was the best that I could think to do. Intention, honest endeavour and naked pleading appeared to be the only essential elements of any petition in order for that petition to succeed beyond my wildest dreams.

There appeared to be no requirement that my supplications be pious. I could speak to God as though he were from the same culture as myself. I never took to calling Him a bollox, but some of our encounters could be quite robust. I would express impatience, frustration, anger with the apparent unwillingness of the situation to yield to His intervention. Was there some problem? What was He waiting for? Was He losing His touch? Invariably, it would emerge that the solution had already been in train, that the apparent failure of the situation to submit had to do, not with a failure or negligence on God's part, but with my inability to let go of my prescriptiveness.

I accept that this will all sound ludicrous and cringe-inducing to rational ears and axiomatic to everyone else. This is why there's almost no point in saying it, other than saying it. And this is not unimportant, because, at the risk of sounding even more ludicrous, I feel obliged to say that the process works better when you're prepared to bear witness to it. God, it seems, likes those He's helped to advertise His services. I'm just reporting the facts.

During the writing of this chapter, I got an email from a woman who had attended a talk I'd given a short time previously in New York. She described for me an incident which had happened to her the previous weekend, walking with her two little boys along the boardwalk by the ocean at Coney Island. 'I was so happy, and was looking for another happy face to pass as I strolled along. I thought, surely someone will at least smile at my two beautiful children sitting side-by-side in their double-stroller. No way. Just one stern face after another. I began to feel very lonely, and I had no other choice but to cry out, "Jesus, please show me your face!" Not even thirty seconds passed when a rather dishevelled man stopped and started waving his hands in front of my children's faces. He said, "This always makes em' laugh. It's no fail." I must admit, if I hadn't asked for it, I might have been a little afraid of the guy. I asked him, "Do you have any children?" He replied: "No, I'm alone in the world. My only son died of a drug overdose in 2002 and then my wife of 41 years died of a broken heart two years later. But you know, the good Lord doesn't want us to go backwards. He wants us to go forwards, so that's what I'm doing!"'

What the woman described is typical of a phenomenon that happens to me almost every day now. I often find that I get a 'sign' or an 'intervention' at moments of importance that are impossible to predict and difficult to pinpoint or analyse. But there is nothing portentous about these moments. They simply happen. They are not like moments in a movie when I am seeking a *deus ex machina* to move my plot along. They are ordinary moments when nothing much is happening. You can come very quickly to take them for granted. Maybe in a part of your brain, no matter how often it has happened before, you think of it as coincidence, but there is a saying in AA for this also: 'Coincidence is a miracle in which God chooses to remain anonymous.'

In some ways this woman described a casual moment, in another sense a pivotal one. It was casual in that there was nothing planned or calculated about it. She had not been looking for anything, least of all for herself. She was happy, in touch with reality and yet unburdened by it. But suddenly her spirit was overcome by weariness and loneliness, though mainly for her children. She did not think of asking for anything but merely gave vent to a deep need within her. This, I find, is how it generally happens. In focusing on our daily wants and needs we forget the deeper need and how much more important it is. Our daily wants and necessities make this need seem all the more acute, but we are not conscious of it. One of the things I have to keep remembering is that, having abdicated from the throne I once occupied as the god of my own existence, I will constantly, if opportunity offers itself, seek to steal back and reinstate myself. Having resigned as the architect of my life, I am constantly seeking to interfere in matters which, strictly speaking, are no longer my responsibility. Then an event occurs which triggers me back into a connection, and the feeling overwhelms me, all the more because I have been keeping it at bay. A moment will arise when I am brought beyond my routine struggles and the kinds of calculation and wheedling that tend to emanate from them. Sometimes it will happen when I am content, in harmony. At other moments it will happen at the other extreme of my emotional spectrum. I will reach a kind of 'last straw' or 'rock bottom' moment, triggered perhaps by something that, in my routine mindset, I regard as trivial. I will spill my coffee down my jacket on top of a series of 'misfortunes' which have dragged me back to myself and my self-obsessions. But the training I obtained from AA prompts me not to respond to this added 'calamity' in the predictable way, but instead to use it as a trigger to surrender. So instead of plunging further into the opening vortex of self-pity, I suddenly find myself laughing at the absurdity of my own catastrophizing. And then the moment of grace will arrive, prompted by this 'trivial' incident. Of course, it is not trivial at all, but touches on what is truly important. Then, always, the phone will ring or someone will turn up – a 'coincidence' will occur. The 'trivial' has brought me beyond myself and my crude everyday-functional view of reality, into what is vital.

I think of this as my 'Help' moment – when I get beyond my immediate agendas and desires to a point where I am confronted with a much deeper sense of need in myself. I then utter this one word, 'Help', and help always comes. And that 'Help' is always set off in me by something apparently unconnected to my concerns of the moment – some added imposition, some tiny grain of worry added to what is already on my plate, as though its very triviality is part of the understanding I need to get to. I am presented with a choice: I can worry about this extra trifle or I can remember that there is One who has all Power and that He is available to me at the blink of an eye.

This kind of thing, what I have just outlined, used to make me shudder with embarrassment and unease. How could an intelligent adult think in such a way? The answer: only if experience has shown you that this is a reasonable way to think. Only if this kind of thing happens so often in your life that it no longer strikes you as odd. The situation the American woman described seemed plausible to me because I had encountered similar moments in my own life, many times in the previous decade. It had in many ways been a difficult decade, largely because of the circumstances surrounding the birth and early life of my daughter, which became a focus of media interest intermittently during the second half of the 1990s. I don't intend to go into it, partly because it is private, partly because it would occasion an unnecessary visitation pain, and partly because I am prohibited from discussing the details by the in camera rule which applies to all family law matters. Suffice it to say that it was a difficult time, in which I awoke on many a morning wishing I could go back to sleep. The overwhelming sense I had in that time was that I had gone to a place beyond human intercession. As many men who become fathers without benefit of marriage were discovering around the same time, I was encountering a culture for which I had no preparation, a system in which the tacit denial of the humanity of single fathers was all but absolute. Those years caused me to question utterly every single value I had absorbed from childhood onwards – justice, truth, decency, fairness. Confronting the legal systems of two jurisdictions I very soon came to realize that there was no earthly place I could go to ask that the natural order be vindicated or decency upheld. For a while it seemed to me that there was only me, that I could rely on nothing but myself and my own resources, wherever I might find them.

I call it my Yosser Hughes period, after the legendary character from *The Boys from the Blackstuff,* Alan Bleasdale's epic television drama from 1982. It was assumed at the time that Bleasdale was writing about 'unemployment', but really he was dealing with redundancy, obsolescence, male despair. At the time I first saw the series, I didn't think that the character of Yosser, in his long black coat, followed by his three children, reciting his insistent mantras: 'Giz a job!'; 'I could do tha!' could ever have anything directly to say to me, but now I found myself thinking of Yosser every day. Yosser was the end of the left-wing illusion, the embodiment of the man who believed that his own essential decency, and the culture of solidarity and social justice which it had tried to create, was enough to see him through. Having come to manhood in the surge of the sixties, he was now stranded on the sandbank of his own optimism. Now he was brought face to face with the limits of what he believed: the failure, essentially, of right-on thinking.

There is a moment in the series when it is possible to say that the hope of those who believed in fellowship, community and togetherness finally died. Yosser, beaten now, finds himself in a confessional, facing, of all things at such a moment, a trendy priest. His children, about to be taken away into care, giggle in the background. He has arrived at the last refuge of the bewildered in an attempt to find words for his situation, but is doomed to remain on his own narrow waveband. The priest is more concerned with putting him at ease, requesting that he drop the formalities. 'Don't worry about the "father",' he says, with blinding irony. 'I'm desperate, father,' says Yosser and he looks beseechingly into the priest's eyes.

Priest: 'Call me Dan. Dan.'

Yosser: 'I'm desperate. Dan.'

Yosser laughs madly and momentarily. He then head-butts the partition between himself and the priest. The scene ends.

It is hard to imagine a more concise or devastating enactment of the despair of a man, or rather a generation of men, caught in the searchlight of their own knowinglessness, their own cultural cleverness, but unable to save themselves.

For most of the second half of the 1990s, I was the demented guy in the long coat. I had a few friends to whom I talked regularly, but most of the people I'd previously associated with began, whether through embarrassment or a sense of awkwardness with the changing nature of my political demeanour, to avoid me.

In that period, I found myself invoking God as I Understood Him on a daily, often an hourly, basis. I cannot put together a sketch of how it all worked out, but work out it did, and I have not the slightest doubt that it worked out because I stopped trying to run things and invited God to take over. My daughter lives in Ireland now, having been born and brought up for the first three years of her life in London. She spends half her time with me and scarcely a day goes by when I don't see or speak to her. She is happy in a way that renders mysterious the foggy events of those years when everything seemed so hopeless. How we got to where we are is a mystery to me, but get here we did.

After this I began to experience things that previously I knew only as phrases. Like the idea, for example, that God is love. One of the things I noticed early on in my own experience of being a father in a situation where I had intermittent contact with my daughter in her early months and years was that the process I would retrospectively describe as the creation of a bond of love was at least as much a rational construction as an emotional phenomenon. I once made the mistake of engaging a very stupid court-appointed child psychiatrist on the subject of love and its true nature, and am not about to make the same mistake in written form. We depend for life on a culture in which profound stupidities masked by sentimentality and piety can acquire a greater moral value than an honest attempt to delve into the complexity of phenomena. But we are speaking here, I hope, among intelligent beings – these truths are not literal, or at least not substantially, or at least not literal in terms that our culture understands. But, in the course of observing my own responses to the development of the father–child relationship with my daughter, it has occurred to me more than once that, without the more prosaic qualities of duty and responsibility, the pearl I now recognize as love might never have developed. And without a more fundamental need in myself, it is doubtful if these qualities of duty and responsibility could have been unearthed from the mire of selfhood that is the inner reality of us all. That need can best be described as a desire to assert a version of myself with which I could be happy, could stand over, could believe in. It has to do with what we call identity, but also with the idea of being perceived as a good and worthy person, which is to say a desire to be loved. And here we possibly perceive how the circle completes itself around what language would have as a tautology: we love so as to be loved. The more we love, the more we attract love (in theory). Love is always, to begin with, in a sense, selfish – it is love as need – but out of that is born the only antidote to selfishness: love as gift. Love, in a sense, is a recycled product, the clear shining outcome of a process in which the tarnished and debased is fed into a crucible of action and giving, to emerge purified, renewed. It takes some of us half our lifetimes (if we're lucky) to discover what the ancients saw clearly: it is far, far better to give than to receive. After decades of seeking in relationships with others the satisfaction of our own needs by the pursuit of this in a direct and unabashed fashion, we may one day stumble upon the discovery that the outcome, for ourselves, is actually far better when we put the other's needs ahead of our own. In doing this we unearth in ourselves a capacity for feeling that all our previous self-seeking had done no more than tease us with. We become airborne. In this way I experience the hard truth behind the AA mantra – 'If I do God's work, He will do mine.' By focusing on something I saw as a duty, I helped into being a collateral process that carried me to a new place.

I attempt to describe this, again, knowing that those who already know what I'm talking about will be bored by the inadequacy of my description and those who don't will simply sigh with cynical impatience. The Reality I address in these moments is not the reality I live with every day, and yet it has something of that reality about it. It is almost on the same frequency but not quite. There is a need for me to adapt myself, to slip ever so slightly off the frequency of everyday reality and acquire a harmony with this Otherness. Of course, this is to put things the wrong way round, for it is everyday reality that is off key, though, being caught within its logic, we think of it as in perfect pitch. This tuning-in cannot be achieved by conscious means, but only by a circuitous route, by first of all disengaging from reality and its concerns and sliding gradually into this other place. And when I am in this place I always know, and always feel safe and understand that nothing but good will happen to me.

If, or when, I let slip in general company that I believe in God, however guardedly or ring-fenced with elaborations, I tend to get two distinct kinds of responses. By 'general company' I mean the kind of people you meet outside of expressly religious contexts, members of the 'general population'. One response is complete silence, which I have come to recognize as the silence of the white-knuckle agnostic. I recognize in such silence the person I used to be when talk of God made me uncomfortable and anxious to distance myself. Deep within me, on encountering such silences, there is a crying need to justify myself, to rebut all the unspoken prejudices and assumptions which I know are firing around the unspeaking head. I have a sense of being revised, of having my CV rewritten, of being squeezed into a smaller box than the one I was squeezed into before I blurted out my confession. Unless invited to elaborate on my beliefs or belief history, I tend to say nothing further on the subject, to surrender myself to the prejudices and the box. For this other person, I accept, I am simply a very naive, perhaps even stupid person who has abandoned reason and regressed to the superstitions of his childhood. So be it.

The other response reminds me of myself also. It is the curiosity of the searching agnostic. This type tends to ask me questions, firstly tentative ones clearly designed to discover if I am simply a 'crawthumper'. If the discussion embraces any content to do with the Catholic Church's 'moral' agenda – divorce, abortion and so forth – and if I have already in the conversation expressed views suggesting broad agreement with this agenda, I will have an uphill struggle to keep my audience engaged. Most episodes of curiosity about God in Ireland tend to short-circuit on any reference to 'traditionalist' or 'conservative' opinions. But if such issues do not break the surface of the discussion, if we can maintain things within socially neutral terms, there is a good chance that I will find myself talking to someone whose life, in religious terms, has broadly been like mine.

If you ask me, everyone's an agnostic sometimes. Who, in the course of their lives, does not doubt? What is faith without doubt anyway? If I believe because I have been told to believe, or because I have suppressed my doubts, and therefore my reason, of what benefit or value is my faith either to me or the God at Whom it is projected? My shift from what I am prepared to call agnosticism to whatever it is I am now is defined not by a shift from unbelief to belief but by a progression from determination not to engage with the possibility of belief to an openness concerning any or every possibility.

My own experience tells me that we can only get to God by dis-believing in Him. I approach the Mystery from the farthest remove, and thereby emphasize my willingness to embrace it utterly. We can only find Him when we have rejected Him and returned, broken, in the despairing hope that we have been mistaken. Scepticism, there-fore, is an essential element of the faith discussion. There is a theory, which I like, that it takes a balance of believers and non-believers to maintain a certain equilibrium in the world. On the one hand, pure earthly logic is essential to survival, but at other times, in other situations, a sense of the religious can become practical as well. Those who argue that religion amounts to stupidity are not merely entitled to their opinions – the rest of us are entitled to hear them. They help us to see where we need to go, and liberate us from the tyranny of piety.

In AA you get introduced to a lot of 'spiritual' books, self-help books, theory of the meaning-of-life books. Some are interesting, some helpful, some all too familiar. For all that AA is about the re-integration of the physical, the mental and the spiritual planes, it is rare to find anything that goes beyond a certain basic depth. Meetings, too, seem to become repetitive. You have heard the same thing so many times that you find yourself telling people that AA has changed, is no longer what it was, when the truth is that it is pre-cisely what it was, and for very good reasons, but that you have changed, moved on, grown new appetites to replace the ones that brought you to AA in the first place.

After a decade or so, I began to feel that I had exhausted the potential of Alcoholics Anonymous to bring me to the places I knew I needed to reach. Then, one day at Dublin Airport, while waiting for a flight to Rome (a secular trip, I have to confess) I was approached by a man who told me he was the 'responsible' (i.e. the head) of the Dublin chapter of a group called Communion and Liberation. His name was Mauro Biondi, and he was a Sicilian who had been living in Ireland for twenty years, having married an Irish-woman and started a family in Dublin. He had been reading some of my articles in the *Irish Times* and wished to invite me to come and speak to the Dublin CL group. I gave him my telephone number and forgot about the encounter. A few weeks later he called me and suggested a date for my talk. I agreed to come, without having the faintest idea what kind of group it was. A few days before the engagement, I called him and asked him what his group might like me to talk about. 'Tell us about your experience,' he said. I took him at his word and told the groups of my journey from childhood faith to agnosticism to the struggle to arrive at a set of beliefs I could call my own. They seemed to like what I said, because subsequently I was invited to speak at a number of CL events, including the 2006 Meeting at Rimini, a fabulous annual happening in one of Italy's most famous Adriatic resorts. But meanwhile, in gratitude for my talk, the Dublin CL group presented me with a number of books by their movement's founder, Father Luigi Giussani, including *The Religious Sense*. I read all the books they gave me and found them difficult and dense. *The Religious Sense* was no less so than the others, but somehow I felt as I was reading it that it was a book that I had been waiting to discover. For here was a book about religion that treated the subject not as something separate from others but as part of the complex tapestry of reality. It was a difficult, densely argued book, full of quotations from artists and writers, clearly written by a man of enormous learning and scintillating intelligence. I had this odd experience of coming across extraordinary moments of revelation and then reading on for pages without any real sense of what I was being told. I read it again, and this time more of the book seemed to show itself.

It is an impossible book to summarize. It is a book about the meaning of life, about the totality of reason, about truth, art, beauty and love. It is a strange book in many ways. It is difficult, first of all, or at least appears to be while you are reading it – all those diagrams and mathematical formulae. Yet, when you think about it afterwards, it appears to be very simple. When you take away all the formulae, citations, diagrams and intricate pursuits of complex thoughts, there is really only one idea in the book. But what an idea! 'All' he is saying really is that we are created to discover the Infinite and that everything we desire is an echo of that imperative. I'm pretty sure I didn't ever hear this before, and yet I already 'knew' it in myself. What I'd heard was that I was created by God to love and obey Him. This might be deemed the same thing, but could also be something quite different, which is how it had struck me most of my life. I had always heard the 'obey' part, and thought the 'love' part was something analogous, a kind of sneaky way of reminding me of my duty to 'put God first'. Giussani told me something slightly different: that God and I are of the same reality and that my destiny is defined by this.

The strangest thing is that he didn't tell me anything I didn't already 'know', in the sense that Giussani simply awoke a dormant sense of reality that was sleeping within me. I think this is why the book is so complex, or why it goes to such lengths to say something 'obvious'. Purely from the perspective of stating its central idea, it doesn't need to be like this, but in order to communicate it to a consciousness trapped in bogus rationality and scepticism and fear, it has to present itself in a manner that speaks to these tendencies. It contains, among so much else, a psychological strategy that is a lever to take the rational mind to a point of simplicity. If you accept its message, the book retrospectively renders its own methodology redundant. I remember almost nothing of it, but after reading it, was re-created in the consciousness that I had as a child, and which communicated itself to me via the simplicities of my perspectives on the world: what I understood about God, my family and the location in which I had found myself, the mystery of Me and the 'Why?' I have always had. Back then, I knew for sure I was here on a search. I knew it intuitively, because I'm pretty sure nobody told me. I had this sense of being alien, of not so much 'not belonging' as still having an imprint of a different reality. But gradually this imprint was worn away – by what we call 'life', what we call 'reality', by religion even – until in the end I couldn't even remember that I was missing it.

The most memorable thing about reading the book has been that it made me think about how everything I was ever told about religion was really only almost true, almost right, almost real. Nothing I was told, in terms of the words of it, now falls away, but everything also reveals itself as being perhaps open to a slightly different meaning, a misleading meaning, a much more puzzling and pointless meaning – an idolatrous meaning. I am amazed by the clarity with which Father Giussani explains what idolatry is. Idolatry, I now know, is everything I have ever been taught, everything I have ever thought, everything I have all my life been trying to get to or escape from.

After reading *The Religious Sense* for the second time, I needed to sit a long time and not think: partly because I had to do a lot of thinking to catch a glimpse of what the author was driving at in the detail of the book, partly because I could not quite understand how he managed to take something so clear and simple out of such an elaborate argument, and partly because I began to sense a need for preparation before I could contemplate starting what I began to suspect was a new outlook on life. I had for some time been open to the idea of constantly remaking myself – up to a point anyway – but now, it seemed, I had 'stumbled' on a direction. The book left me so animated by a renewed sense of my connection to the Beyond that I was for a time afraid to open it again, in case the feeling might be an illusion.

I no longer feel it adequate, in response to probing, to emphasize that I 'believe' in God, though sometimes, for pragmatic reasons, I will confine myself to this response or even a lesser one. I know God exists. To not believe in God would for me be like refusing to believe in the weather, or in the concept of love, or perhaps in air. It would be like the daffodil denying the sun. Today, God is part of my life in a way He never was before, even as a child. I am certain of His presence and His love. I know these to be physical realities, proximate phenomena that I have access to at all times.

This, in turn, has changed my very nature, not absolutely, but in a dramatic way nonetheless. I don't manage to retain a connection with this reality all the time. Sometimes, through tiredness or disappointment or fear, or perhaps because of a feeling that I have through my behaviour strayed beyond the bounds of God's love, I fall prey to scepticism and become, briefly, the person I used to be. On the other hand, I have, at times, or all the time in some part of my head, a wholly different response to reality, the condition that Ernest Kurtz diagnosed so well in *Not-God*, the condition that drove me to drink, and which all the time reduces part of me to being a spectator at my own life, even when I am immersed in that life.

The meaning of the word 'relativism', much bandied about by theologians nowadays, has never been clear to me. It's a word lots of 'conservative' voices use nowadays to signify the evasion of Truth, the splintering of reality and the obsession with subjectivity, but it always seems to me to be a short-circuit, a device that ultimately sucks the possibility of meaning out of the discussion.

The accusation of relativism nearly always seems to come from a particular ideological viewpoint and is levelled against others. But the thing that strikes me most forcibly about it is that, whatever relativism is – and I can see the condition vaguely, occasionally clearly – it is something I suffer from, something that infects me like a virus, whose purpose is to tear my consciousness asunder. In my need to understand everything, I fall into the established ways of sorting and classifying, categorizing and prioritizing, and at the back of my mind am guilty of the ultimate idolatry which is the, yes, presentiment that, one day, I, or someone on my behalf, and acknowledging my contribution, will know Everything, and therefore will have transcended what I feel is my transitional acceptance of Mystery. I have this in me from my teens, and also, of more recent awakening, its antithesis. In another part of my being (I was about to write 'my head' when I realized that the force I speak of here comes from elsewhere – heart, gut, spirit, who knows?), I have a contrary impulse, which is to do with my nothingness. I pluck out words that seem to relate to this feeling: humility, powerlessness, dependence, obedience, surrender. And this feeling is beset by all kinds of collateral emotions: a disgust of humility, a terror of my powerlessness, an impatience with my dependence, a resistance to obedience, and an absolute physical block against the idea of surrender. So, I feel at once the humility and the egotistical disgust it provokes, the powerlessness and the sense of helplessness it unleashes, the freedom of surrendering but also the dizziness that arises from having let go my grip on the controls of my life, and so forth.

But, because I have strategies for dealing with this condition, it rarely lasts. I welcome it as another part of the reality that was created in me. I breathe and it goes away.

It is difficult to describe this new reality of mine without stumbling across one of the many semantic tripwires which modern society has installed as, it often seems, a deliberate attempt to deter expressions of belief. There is nothing pious about my belief. In my outward personality, as I have tried to stress, I haven't changed very much at all. I still do much the same things I always did, including things I have previously found to be mistakes. I swear as much, if not more, than I did. My belief has almost nothing to do with being 'good'. If I am 'good' in any sense, it is not because of my new-found belief, although it has undoubtedly to do with the roots of that belief in the religion of my childhood.

My faith is more radical than any of that. It is, you might say, a technology for living, a means of approaching reality on a daily basis in order to make the best of my life. This, of course, implies pursuing a 'goodness' of sorts, but it is not a pious goodness. It is not intended for show, nor can it be measured in my adherence to rules.

In what sense can I say that my arrival at this point was as a result of my reason? In the sense that my reason is the totality of my capacity to comprehend, which includes, as well as logic and intelligence, my emotions, my intuition and my desire. In *The Religious Sense*, Giussani quotes a book I have not read, by Claude Tresmontant, called *Towards the Knowledge of God* (Baltimore: Helicon, 1961). 'According to the Gospels,' wrote Tresmontant, 'belief is the discovery and understanding of the truth that is proposed to us. To the child who is learning how to swim we explain that because of natural laws there is no reason to be afraid, and if he will only make a few simple movements he will be able to swim. But the child is perhaps still afraid. He shrinks back, and does not seem to believe us. But finally the moment comes when he experiences for himself [that] what he was told is really possible, after all. He believes and now he is able to swim. In this case, it cannot be said that faith is opposed to reason.'

I discovered for myself the accuracy of this analogy.

By the time I reached my forties, it had been so long since I had learned to do anything that I hadn't been able to do before that I had forgotten entirely what learning was like. I remembered in an abstract way learning to ride a bicycle. I recalled, vaguely, that I went from not being able to do it to doing it in pretty much a moment. But I had no memory of the process, other than fuzzy Proustian flashes. That was when I was ten. In the meantime, I didn't appear to have learned anything. Perhaps I tell a lie: I must, at some point, have learned to type, but even this, although I am doing it to write this, is debatable. When I shift momentarily from focusing on what I am typing to focusing on the typing, I realize that I have lost most of what I learned when I sat the typing book up in front of an old Remington on the kitchen table. I get by in typing, as I get by in Spanish, Italian and Irish and changing a baby's nappy. But I do not feel, and do not think I ever felt, a sense of exhilaration about having actually learned any of these things. There was no moment, I don't believe, in which I moved from not knowing how, to knowing how. Swimming, therefore, was a first. Or perhaps a first in my living memory. I remember a time when I was not merely unable to swim but had what I now regard as a laughable fear of water. I remember a time, not long ago, when I was afraid of standing up in three feet of water. I remember a time when even looking at three feet of water filled me with unease. And now, without question, I am able to swim. I am not able to swim as well as other people, but I am able to swim very well by the standards of my own past hopes and dreams. I am able to swim well enough to know that I can keep getting better. This is pretty much how it is with God also.

When I set out, not merely to learn to swim, but to write for a glossy monthly about the process of learning to swim, I had a sense that swimming was a metaphor for life. Before long, I became convinced that life is a metaphor for swimming.

I have known for most of my half-century of life that, even though we shared a name, water was my enemy, perhaps my worst one. It was a place, thing, entity, element, I had avoided since our first encounter. I remember it being cold and unfriendly in a way I took quite personally.

We had a swimming pool in Castlerea, which was unusual in small west of Ireland towns at the time. It was an open-air, unheated pool that opened in the summer months only. I first went there with my class when I was eight or nine, and didn't go back for nearly four decades. I remember that first time getting into what I anticipated would be an alien environment and having my prejudices confirmed with every flinch down the steps. I remember the water as life threatening. I remember how it tried to squeeze the life out of me – literally a sense of the air being compressed upwards through my chest and out through the orifices of my head. I remember the smell of the chlorine, which would become synonymous forever afterwards with the concept of fear.

It is only in recent years, after my little girl came along and gave me something to fret about besides myself, that I began to consider the matter again, in particular to explore the theory that the whole problem may have been in my head. Not being completely immune to rationality, even in matters of terror, I could not avoid being occasionally struck by the fact that other people did not feel about water as I did. They seemed to quite enjoy it, to trust it, to give themselves to it without much thought. I would watch swimmers for signs of imminent asphyxiation, or horror, or trembling, and see only laughing faces. The worst they seemed to feel was the odd laugh-making shiver.

I remember, too, how seductive it was, on hot summer days, when the shouts of other children rose up from behind the concrete wall of the swimming pool, an oasis in the Castlerea Demesne. I remember how, when I longed to be cool, the water would present itself in an altogether different light, how it would twinkle and smile, how it would seem to suspend its threat to kill me, and instead offer me an embrace that I could, in some part of me, succumb to and go on living.

The very phrase 'going for a swim' seemed to contain in it a promise of something that I knew was deeply pleasurable but yet beyond my grasp. I would fantasize about swimming, imagine that I could do it, that it was as easy as it looked, imagine even that I actually knew how to do it. But the water of my fantasy and the water of reality seemed to be two completely different substances. I needed only to look into its depths to know that my fantasy was a seductive lie, that in real life the water would draw me in and then draw me down to its evil heart.

Over the years, I made a couple of desultory attempts to learn to swim, but with dismal results. I had returned to the water, if only to stand there or walk around the shallow end. But I had at least discovered that the sensation of asphyxiation was to do with the cold rather than the water. I got to almost like going into the water, as long as my head stayed well clear of it. I would lose myself in the crowd and pretend to myself that I looked like I was about to go under or had just surfaced from an invigorating swim. Nobody seemed to notice, perhaps because they weren't thinking about me as much as I was thinking about myself.

As I approached my first half-century, frustrated by my inability to keep up with my then almost seven-year-old daughter, I signed up for lessons at a south Dublin swimming pool. The instructor was a woman of mature years, who kept telling me, as though this assurance would be sufficient to banish all my disquiet, that I would not drown. 'You'll float,' she would declare confidently, and then invite the other learners (all much younger and more advanced) to have a good laugh at my ineptitude. Once she tried to kick the legs from under me. 'You won't drown,' she shouted, as I went under, taking the precaution of grabbing her head as I went. In fact, I nearly drowned the both of us, and I was immediately banished to do a crocodile walk in the baby pool, from which position I would occasionally look up to see my tormentor drawing my punitive humiliation to the attention of some newcomer.

The water terrified me. I would be visited by full-blown technicolour images of my dead body floating upwards on the water. Phrases like 'drowning man', 'swollen features' and 'bulging eyes' would spring spontaneously into my consciousness, as though from a news report of my death. At the moment, for example, of throwing myself forward, I would be visited by an image of my body with a crowd around it, and I would stumble in mid take-off and collapse in an embarrassment of splashes, causing anyone nearby to look around for a lifeguard.

I think the water is the measure of my own lack of faith in myself.

Water fills things, takes their shape. Water is the shape and substance, as well as the symbol, of the untamed world that frightens me
still. It isn't simply that I'm afraid of water, but that water is everything I'm afraid of. By conquering it, I'm conquering myself,
reducing the quantum of my fears by just so much.

As an adult watching my child in the water, I have long had a sense
that, although I remain her protector, she has much less fear than I
do. It is as if, because I have lived a long time, my fears fill the pool,
whereas a child sees mainly water. But the main problem seems to be
to do with spontaneity. A child seems to be able to survey the act and
logic of swimming and replicate it almost by instinct, whereas an
adult has to construct it mechanically and then convert it into a
natural movement. For example, when I started to learn the hand
movements for the front crawl, I spent quite a long time doing
something that might be termed 'swimming-by-numbers'. Left hand
stretched out, right behind; left hand back, right hand forward,
being careful to clear the water; left hand forward, etc. There was a
distinct and by no means short period when I was doing this with no
physical sense of its purpose or meaning. It was a series of motions
which I'd learned off, and because of this, I often lost concentration,
forgot where I was and ended up floundering. I had a sense that,
somewhere in there was the idea of forward propulsion, which I
rather abstractly connected to the motion of the hands going backwards. But for a while this concept remained utterly alien to the
sequence I was trying to perform. If I tried to shift my concentration
from the swimming-by-numbers sequence to the idea of forward
propulsion, I would either lose my rhythm or forget about kicking
my feet, both of which would have similar kinds of consequences.
The connection between the two came only with repeated practice,
mostly with no sense of progress. Like a lot of things in the process
of learning to swim, it just happened one day when I wasn't thinking
about it. I had a sense that I was, for the first time, consciously pro-
pelling myself forward, and that the rhythm of the sequence was
remaining intact of its own volition. My movements appeared, for
the first time, spontaneous. I was doing what my daughter, having
overcome her fear, had done at her first attempt.

Faith returned to me in much the same way. It did not descend on me as a blinding light, but came gradually through trial and error. In a sense I had to become a child again, and gradually my skills blurred into something that might loosely be called swimming.

So with my relationship with God. It has struck me many times that we are born with a sense of God but become convinced by the world and by ourselves that it is too good to be true. It takes years of punishment to reduce us to a condition whereby we see no option but to rediscover this lost sense in ourselves.

Water is a good metaphor too for the reality that faith makes known to me. When I go into the water, I know I am entering a different world. The world I am familiar with remains close by, but its reassurance resides purely in the knowledge that I can, by means of a mechanical movement I've found to work, return to it more or less at will. The dry-land world I'm used to, I know, has no jurisdiction underwater. It cannot intervene, cannot intercede. In a sense, when I enter the water – I mean when I go under it – I abandon something I usually take for granted. Not hope, I think, but perhaps faith of the kind I am used to exercising on dry land. There, usually, my faith is a kind of bridge built of experience over the river of fear. I have a general sense of what may happen and why. I know, for instance, that when I place one foot in front of the other, I will move forward. I know that when I turn the steering wheel to the left, the car will turn with it. There must have been a time when these things did not appear axiomatic, but I cannot remember it. Underwater, I require a different kind of faith, because the rules are different. The apparatus I have used for anticipating danger on land is not merely useless, but is actually problematic. For quite a while, as I tried to learn to float, I found myself over-reacting to the movements of my body underwater, the lack of control causing me to panic and spring clumsily down to my feet and up to the air. It took me a while to understand that I was in the arms of the water much more than I was used to being in the arms of the atmosphere above. I was bringing my land-based assumptions, reactions, anticipations and anxieties into the pool with me. One of the sensations I would feel was analogous, up to a point, to the feeling of slipping on a patch of ice. I had this feeling all the time underwater, and for a while responded to it as I had been used to on land. 'Knowing' I was 'falling', I would try to correct the fall, and at the same time realize that the attempt was hopeless. This would bring on a panic attack, which would cause me to verticalize myself pre-emptively. On land, my response would have been more or less correct: I had felt myself falling, therefore I was. On water, however, the same level of fear would be the response to the perfectly natural movements of my body in the water. I had to teach myself to ignore the signals of fear far beyond a point where I felt safe, and delay my response until I had time to observe the outcome. The answer resided in perseverance, repetition. I would consciously decide to ignore the fear for perhaps a few extra seconds each time, until I learned a new kind of response to a situation I thought I recognized but was confusing with something from a different world entirely.

So it is too with the relationship between faith and unbelief. The world of faith is a completely different world from the one without it. It may look and feel similar, or connected, but this is a trick of the light. Once you even begin to believe that there is a Presence which is greater than everything, nothing ever looks to you as it did before.

Swimming, I find, is about faith, and therefore offers a way of talking about faith that is uncontaminated by prejudices and icon-ographies and linguistic tics. The water provides a perfect metaphor for the faithless reality because it makes visible the otherwise spectral fear that accompanies most, if not all, human beings in the very core of their beings.

The logic of my fear of water, I eventually worked out, was not so much about drowning, as about falling. All my life I had watched people swim, but from the edge of the pool, from above them, thinking of them 'down there' in the water. For a while, as I began to learn to swim, I thought of myself in that way, and imagined that I was afraid I would go under the water and drown. But then one day it struck me that what I was afraid of was falling. This gave me a new way of looking at myself: standing on solid ground and throwing myself into the space in front of me. I was afraid I would not be able to fly, because I knew I could not. But in the water, I could 'fly' for as long as I kept that fear at bay, which is to say for as long as I believed in my ability to 'fly'.

And so it is with belief in God. Previously, I was terrified of a world I didn't trust to support me. I feared everything, mistrusted everything. Now I accept, as a matter of fact, that I am part of reality, that I can throw myself into the stuff of the everyday and be sure it will embrace my surrender. I cannot think this process into being. I can only do it. It depends on action based on trust, and feeling based on a state of harmony with the world, which can also be called grace.

# — 6 —

# The Hole in the Doughnut

In the early part of 2007, as I was nearing the end of the writing of this book, the Taoiseach Bertie Ahern made an interesting, if slightly unexpected, speech about the status of faith in Irish society. Speaking in Dublin Castle at the opening of a 'structured dialogue with churches, faith communities and non-confessional bodies', Mr Ahern had warned of the dangers of 'aggressive secularism' and the tendency of public discourse to sideline or disparage religion as something outmoded or dangerous. 'So much of what is happening within our society and in the wider world is bound up with questions of religion, religious identity and religious belief', he said, 'that governments which refuse or fail to engage with religious communities and religious identities risk failing in their fundamental duties to their citizens.'

This, considering the secularized nature of the discourse into which the Taoiseach was seeking to advance his analysis, was radical stuff. Usually when we hear talk in the public square about a 'right' to religious belief, it is in the context of the need for public 'tolerance' of faith and religious practice. The implication is seldom far from the surface of such platitudes that, of course, whereas those who engage in such superstitions are to be 'tolerated', they are also to be regarded as engaging in a near-obsolescent and unmodern activity. Irish society increasingly seems merely to put up with people who believe in God because such 'tolerance' is part of the liberal ideology of the moment.

It had been some time since I had heard a public figure identify precisely why this is such a dangerous trend. We are suffering at present, the Taoiseach said, from 'a form of aggressive secularism which would have the State and State institutions ignore the importance of the religious dimension. They argue that the State and public

123

policy should become intolerant of religious belief and preference, and confine it, at best, to the purely private and personal, without rights or a role within the pubic domain. Such illiberal voices would diminish our democracy. They would deny a crucial dimension of the dignity of every person and their rights to live out their spiritual code within a framework of lawful practice, which is respectful of the dignity and rights of all citizens. It would be a betrayal of the best traditions of Irish republicanism to create such an environment.'

Mr Ahern here expressed something that no politician or public figure had articulated for a generation, and few clergymen had managed to say so well. Usually, when the subject of religion is broached in public, it is either by way of pious invocation or derisory dismissal. Catholic bishops, for example, frequently speak about the importance of religious faith, but they tend, in doing so, to suggest that faith and religion should be embraced as a kind of duty, perhaps even a duty to them and their church, or, in the personal context, as a guarantor of goodness. The Taoiseach was saying something altogether more interesting and profound: that human beings have a deep need for what religion offers, and that the right to practise it is therefore a fundamental human entitlement.

I wrote my column in the *Irish Times* the following week in support of Mr Ahern's position. Although the current fashion for atheism, agnosticism and secularism tends to convey the idea that religion is merely a hangover from outmoded tradition, I observed, there is considerable evidence that it is, in fact, a natural and essential element of the human psyche: 'The cleverality of the present moment tends to dismiss what our forebears took for granted: that we are born with a longing for what is Beyond, and that this longing is as real in us as the sexual instinct or the sense of smell. Disparaged it may be, but tradition knew something about us that we seek to deny: there is a religious dimension inherent in the human being, faith comes from within, and without these we are less than human. This surely tells us that the importance of religion goes far beyond issues of morality and identity, extending also to hope, meaning and freedom. The world on its own does not offer sufficient hope to carry the average human being through an average life. The baubles of the marketplace do not for long serve to quiet the longing in the human heart. And the promise of earthly freedom fails to address the issue of how we are to free ourselves from our instincts, our weaknesses, our egos and our selfishness.'

As we observe our society plunging into the secular paradise promised by the liberal ideologues who triumphed over the custodians of tradition, we observe also the manifestation of the many baneful symptoms of this shift. Alcohol, drugs, rampant consumerism, sex crimes and countless related phenomena tell us that there is something in the human being that is voided by secular, material society. Increasingly, our society manifests an erosion of hope, a misdefinition of freedom and a collapse of meaning, and all these phenomena are directly related to the disappearance from our culture of what we know of as religion. This is not simply because the Catholic Church has lost the authority to tell us what to do, but because, in the absence of a religious consciousness, there is, ultimately, no hope, no meaning and no freedom.

The following week, as almost invariably happens when someone broaches this or related subjects, the letters page of the *Irish Times* was filled for several days with correspondence on the subject. It is remarkable that, in a society which constantly tells itself that it is losing its religion, this alleged loss is attended with far more discussion than ever attended the uncritical embrace of Catholicism which preceded it. In the main, my personal in-tray reflected the readers' letters published over several days. Some were supportive, some critical, some both; a few demanded apologies (mainly for my alleged assertion that those who did not believe in God were 'less than human'), and one or two opened windows I had never noticed before. A couple of emails, as well as some of the published letters, sought to set atheists up as the latest marginalized minority, demanding retractions of the 'offence' they had taken from my article. I responded the following week by saying that for us to be persuaded by this logic, which had circumscribed discussion of virtually anything involving a so-called 'lifestyle choice', would be to become the accomplices of our own gravediggers.

I also heard from quite a few pleasant and interesting atheists, several of whom assured me that they disagreed with me about God but thought it unfair of me to lump them in with liberals. This alerted me to one possible deficiency in my understanding of things. The inevitable sociological shorthand one tends to employ in seeking to describe social patterns in a newspaper column can often lead to incorrect conflations, and it struck me that I had indeed been guilty of such a sin in tarring atheists, secularists and liberals with the same brush. Although the Irish media tend to convey an unrelenting sense of attack on God and the Church, it was perhaps unfair to convinced atheists to associate them in a blanket way with this phenomenon. In fact, one of the core problems with atheism is that it is a solitary business, by definition an unclubbable calling. On reflection, I would say that most of what we recognize as secularism in the public domain in Ireland is so transparently lacking in any philosophical rootedness as to reveal itself as merely a neurotic response to a bad experience of Catholicism. What distinguishes this from the stream of apparently genuine atheism that appears to exist in the private domain is that it is driven fundamentally by the energy deriving from a collective backlash against the Church. Attacking the Catholic bishops, ridiculing Catholic theology and rejecting the dominion of Catholicism in the social life of Ireland is the main focus of this, the dominant ideology in Irish public life now.

Judging from the response I received from the atheistic community, the emerging trend towards outright atheism is something quite different. It is the response in the private dimension to the erosion of this public culture and may reflect some kind of snapshot of the next stage. Many of those who wrote describing themselvas as atheists (there were none who used the word 'agnostic') made mention of a bad experience of Catholicism also, but almost as an ancient memory. They had moved on to a new place, in which they had found peace, but which for me seemed like the beginning of death.

In writing that there is a religious dimension inherent in the human being, that faith 'comes from within', and that without these we are less than human, I had not wished to imply that those calling themselves atheists were 'less than human'. I had meant, rather, that – and this may seem even more offensive – it is not possible for a human being to deny his or her religious dimension successfully. To do so, I wrote subsequently, 'makes approximately the same sense as a daffodil trying to deny the existence of the sun'. We are of God, made in His likeness. He (or, if you must be pedantic, She/It) is our identity and our destiny. The remarkable thing I picked up from this brief correspondence was that many atheists seemed to be closer to understanding this than most of us who had simply sleepwalked most of our lives through what we had been taught to regard as a spiritual existence. These non-believers seemed to have looked more closely at reality than those who had swallowed whole the prescriptions of organized religion, and in many cases the intensity of their searching could be described as, well, religious.

'You claim', one reader wrote, 'that without religion there is "no hope, no meaning and freedom". Naturally I cannot speak for the entire planet, but as an Atheist I promise, I live with hope, I live with meaning and most of all I live with freedom. Freedom because I am no longer tortured with images of burning in hell as I was as a child. It has been the most liberating experience of my life when I finally understood that God and Religion is nothing but a superstitious hangover from a more base time. I feel more connected to this universe now than I ever did as a believing Christian. I suspect, perhaps in error, that you don't really understand Atheists. You don't see that Atheism is not simply a position of moral or mental laziness. The default position for society today is to believe in God, to believe in religion. Almost every child is brought up that way in some form or another. They either get it drummed in by their family or else society at large. It is a long road for most Atheists to reach the spiritual awareness of not believing in God. They tend to think about it a lot and reach their conclusions after much research and self-enquiry. How many of the billions of religious can we say that of today?'

It seems to me that, for all the validity of his observations, this man had mistaken his negative reaction to religion as a philosophical understanding of the totality of reality. Because those who claimed to speak for God were weak or bad, everything they said must be wrong. He claimed to feel hope, to have meaning and to know freedom, and yet his hope, meaning and freedom were defined, in his own description, by his sense of escape from an imprisoning sense of religion. It seemed not to occur to him that his experience of Catholicism had had nothing to do with faith, religion or God, but was, in common with many such experiences, an encounter with earthly power.

This erroneous rejection of an erroneous religiosity is deeply damaging to our children's chances of peace and happiness. Atheists may be likeable, interesting people, but I have a difficulty with the proposition that they have anything coherent to offer either society or posterity. While it may well be possible for an individual to live a hopeful, meaningful and free life without God, there is no evidence whatever to suggest that this can be achieved by a society. And the ultimate irony is that the 'hope' atheists claim to feel may well derive not from their own philosophical resting place but from the background radiation of hope deriving from the residual effects of intense cultural faith. In other words, whereas it is possible for an individual to survive quite happily without God in the midst of many who continue to believe – you might say piggy-backing on the faith of others – it is not possible for a society to survive without a critical mass of believers.

To be 'an agnostic' in modern Ireland means several things, of which an attitude towards God is perhaps the least evident. Agnosticism is a cast of mind which you acquire as a way of functioning in the culture. It begins as a reaction to, a rejection of, the Catholic Church, which in turn has to do with liberating yourself, especially to do with what church personnel refer to as 'moral' issues. This mainly means, in one way or another, sex. There seems, too, to be a consensus among the organizers of the public conversation, otherwise known as the media, that it is permitted to talk about God so long as you implicitly agree with the official consensus that the whole thing is nonsense anyway but that it remains an interesting historical peculiarity and therefore a legitimate talking point. We are so embedded in the secular logic that it is difficult even to see how strong its grip is upon us. Secularism has become invisible, not merely to the secular, but also to those who continue to believe but also seek to live in the secular world.

In *An Intelligent Person's Guide to Modern Ireland*, I wrote about an atheist friend of mine who observed to me some years previously that Irish liberals, while never claiming to be disbelievers, equally did not present themselves as believers. 'This man, who has no difficulty stating his profound view that God does not exist,' I wrote, 'takes a great interest in Catholic theology, primarily he says, because religion and its influence is impossible to escape from, but also because even atheists have a spiritual yearning to understand the mystical and mysterious. Perhaps, I offered, Irish indifference to such matters is the consequence of a deep faith which allows us to take them for granted. But no: he had noticed, he told me, that whenever he brought up the subject of God with his fellow Irishmen and Irishwomen, they tended to fidget, make jokes, giggle nervously and look at their shoes. For a country which has made so much play of its Catholicism, he remarked, it is strange that so few people respond to such promptings in a way as to suggest to him that they believe in the existence of God.'

It is difficult to get to the bottom of the extent to which this syndrome corresponds to an actual social phenomenon. Public discussion certainly reflects this sense of embarrassment, with most talk concerning religion or Catholicism tending to focus on the political and social aspects, rather than issues of faith or God.

Spiritual matters are treated by mainstream media as parallel realities meriting condescension or, at best, disinterested respect. While substantial coverage is accorded to church politics, Church–State relations and theological discussion, these are mainly treated as pertaining to a discrete reality, with the language and assumptions of faith being notably absent from media treatment of more general issues. It is as though the consensus of media is that faith is a load of baloney, but a certain service must be maintained for those clinging to superstition.

These trends largely followed the pattern established by the separation of Church and State that occurred piecemeal from the 1960s onwards, generally formalized in a series of constitutional changes which made this separation explicit. These changes were partly a reaction to an earlier time in which religious pieties and assumptions were unquestioningly treated as primary elements of public thought.

The first subtext of growing secularization in Ireland, therefore, has to do with what might be called 'the progressive dynamic'. Under the rules of this agenda, faith is a measure of superstition, and therefore backwardness. When the subject of faith is discussed in public, what is at stake is never the condition of faith from a perspective of benevolence or concern, but rather its decline as an indicator of 'progress'. Those who supervise such discussions are invariably atheists or agnostics who, though they 'take an interest' in the religious practices of their fellows, are always anxious to distance themselves from anything except the political implications of religion and faith. Such people – and they seem to represent the great majority of those who lead such discussion in the public square – deliver discussion of faith, practice and devotion in much the way a vegetarian waiter might serve up a medium-rare steak.

The second subtext relates very much to the first, and has to do with the use of political concepts to attack not merely the Catholic Church but, implicitly, the idea of religion and the phenomenon of belief. Thus, in the past couple of decades, the various scandals besetting the Irish Church have been used continuously as weapons with which to assault not merely the institutional church but also the faith of those who continue to practise and believe. Often there is no occasion to quarrel with the import of these discussions in so far as they relate to wrongdoing by particular priests and other church personnel. But this is generally only the beginning of the discussion, which invariably goes on to examine the alleged implications of such wrongdoing for the condition of Irish faith. In all these discussions, the concept of faith is deemed to be inextricable from the fate not merely of Catholicism but also of the Catholic Church in Ireland. And the Church, in turn, is invariably deemed to be coterminous with the church personnel of the present moment. All analyses, then, are predicated on a series of links between faith, the Church, the present-day hierarchy and the events which are emphasized and re-emphasized in the context of alleged implications for the decline of faith in Irish society.

It is sometimes possible to observe that many of these connections are not valid outside the crude political framework in which they are invariably rehearsed, but to do so invites the suspicion that you are trying to defend the Church from another angle. Occasionally I have sought to put the argument like this: to suggest that, whereas the state of health of the Irish Catholic Church may be an interesting and sometimes depressing story, it has little or nothing to do with the condition of Irish faith, and still less to do with the likely future of Catholicism in Irish society. Faith is not a product for which demand ebbs and flows, and, contrary to the impression given in so many media discussions, the Catholic Church is not the manufacturer – beleaguered by scandal and competition – of such a product. The relationship between faith and Catholicism in Ireland is a hugely complex one, and the fate of one does not necessarily depend on the fate of the other. By this I do not mean that 'the Faith' could necessarily survive the collapse of the Church, but that the futures of both Faith and Church are not coterminous concepts.

Because the secularists are embarrassed to talk about God, they refuse to think beyond the relationship between 'the faithful' and the Church, and this purely in its momentary, transient incarnation. But the animation of the faith of Irish people depends far less on the temporary condition of the Catholic Church than on the connection between the people and God. And this, paradoxically, can become far stronger in times of turmoil and travail. There is, then, another way of looking at all this: that the faith of the people is capable of renewing the Church, and that increasing numbers of people are already becoming alert to the urgent necessity of this occurring. But this is not something that can be contemplated in public, still less measured or monitored in terms of its beneficial aspects, while the custodians of the discussion remain mainly those who, being without any faith of their own, are implacably hostile to the condition in other people.

Agnosticism is not a theological position. It is, at bottom, a position that has been arrived at mainly as a reaction, without much thought, by following the line of least resistance. Culturally, in Ireland, one is rarely, if ever, explicitly recognized as an agnostic. Rather it becomes obvious that one is not a devout believer. If one does not go about the place asserting belief, agnosticism is assumed, which is to say that it is taken for granted that one agrees with the prevailing consensus against the Church and God.

There are a number of benefits the individual stands to gain from this, the most important of which is an unearned reputation for cleverness. To volunteer statements indicating belief in God is to risk being seen as simple-minded or worse, by a culture in which these reflexes are built into the fabric of public thought. To be an agnostic is to be smart by default, because other agnostics tend to promote your cleverness in return for you promoting theirs. To believe and to state your beliefs publicly is to have to stand on your own two feet, to have everything you say on whatever subject coloured and diminished by virtue of your known belief in God.

In truth, there is no such thing as a completely rational human being, because rationality seems to demand total knowledge and understanding. Even if we could calculate the totality of human knowledge, it would still amount to but a tiny, notional fraction of what may (or may not) be knowable. And each human being, regardless of achievement or brilliance, has access only to an infinitesimal amount, even of what is already known. Anyone who lives in an advanced Western society is dependent to a high degree on scientific achievements he does not understand, and is therefore a passenger on the knowledge and achievement of others, living and dead. Agnostics who write letters to the *Irish Times* from what is presented as a scientific-rational perspective usually do so in rooms lit and heated by processes they barely understand, on machines they couldn't fix in the event of a breakdown. What's rational or scientific about that? Western agnosticism is not knowledge-based, but merely clings to the *idea* of science, taking out a mortgage on the putative future discoveries that agnostics assume, on the basis of a relatively negligible grasp of what is currently known, will vindicate their unbelief. Modern society simply invites us to replace one form of faith with another, and this is as prone to fundamentalist expostulation as any form of traditionalism.

And Irish secularists are motivated far less by even the idea of a rational-scientific worldview than by a sense of disappointment with a deity whom they have relatively recently given up on. Perhaps because of their treatment at the hands of this deity's earthly representatives, or the perceived failure of their own religious practice in early life, they have developed an attitude towards religious faith that is closer to hatred than to unbelief. Their scorn for believers confirms the existence of something less rational than the repudiation of superstition which they profess.

Secular fundamentalism may therefore exist disproportionately as a symptom of Irish lapsed-Catholicism. Its primary symptom is a refusal of the authority of God, less because self-styled secularists have discovered God to be implausible than because they resent the idea of divine authority. The issue is not rationalism, but arrogance, or, more specifically, lack of humility. It is not that secularists are convinced that God does not exist, but that they cannot bear to think of being subordinate to a deity who made their lives possible. It is hard to imagine anything less rational.

It is true, of course, that the inability of science to explain everything does not in itself legitimize religion. But it surely cautions modesty on the part of those who propose that science is the best, if not the only, way forward.

Faith is eminently rational, not because its tenets are empirically demonstrable, but because it has worked for millennia in providing meaning in a reality that might otherwise have been insufficient to sustain human life. No atheistic state has ever been known to survive beyond the third generation, which indicates that materialism is insufficient sustenance for the human spirit. Usually such societies fail spectacularly, declining into mass depression, addiction and spiritual malaise. In deciding that agnosticism can work for the individual, we may frequently overlook the extent to which that individual is buffered and protected by the level of transcendent beliefs surviving in the surrounding culture. In this sense, the secular-agnostic may, as well as piggy-backing on the scientific achievements of others, be a parasite on the faith of the very believers he derides.

Every so often there develops in the public square of modern Ireland a cultural panic concerning the apparent tension between, on the one hand, the demands of a 'traditional' cultural outlook based on the particularity of Catholicism, and those of a more 'pluralist' ethic reflecting the changing nature of Irish society today. The pretext can shift, but the substance is constant: a confused desire to jettison something that feels uncomfortable and suggests itself as superfluous, but which at the same time seems to have deep roots in the ground around us. Sometimes this discussion will take the form of a controversy about the religious ethos of the education system (still overwhelmingly Catholic), or perhaps why references to God remain in the preamble to the Constitution. Every couple of years, there is a debate about why we still have the angelus on radio and television every day at noon and 6 p.m. The odd thing is that each recurrence of this debate conveys a sense that it is happening for the first time. The same things are said each time, but in a manner suggesting that they have only just popped into someone's mind. Nothing is ever resolved and soon the discussion is dropped, only to surface again in a different context a few months later.

The main basis for these intermittent objections to the angelus is that it is 'sectarian'. Because it is a ritual belonging to a specific religion; that is, the majority religion – it is deemed not merely to exclude others but even to insult them. The time has come, someone asserts, to replace it with a more 'inclusive' ritual. The trouble is that, when the question of what is meant by 'inclusive' is pursued, the only definition that emerges is one implying a necessity for some vague ritual that will be equally meaningless to everyone.

When I was an altar boy, the ringing of the angelus in the local church in Castlerea was perhaps the most sacred of the roles which could be performed by those without benefit of ordination. The sacristan who was responsible for this task on a daily basis at home in Castlerea was Jack Cassidy, a man of the utmost punctiliousness, not to say punctuality. I never knew Jack to be more than a couple of seconds late with the first ring. No matter where you were, within as much as five miles of town, it was certain that at noon and at six you would hear the angelus ring on time. Leaving aside its significance in the Catholic faith, the angelus bell was an extraordinary few moments twice every day, if only because Jack's almost superhuman exactitude, based on duty, deep reverence and personal faith, reminded us that there was something bigger and more constant than ourselves. And it is precisely this – that the angelus reminds us that there is something greater than ourselves – that provokes these intermittent attempts to put an end to it. Although the advocates of such a change invariably come up with all kinds of arguments about minorities feeling offended by such majoritarian practices and rituals, the truth is that nobody is offended by these rituals except those who were born and raised as Irish Catholics and who have rejected this belief-system, or at least assert that they have. This is the paradox of pluralism: it champions everything except existing reality. It is in favour of everything that exists someplace else, and believes that what exists in the here and now should move over and make space for what 'might' or 'should' be. This invites not diversity but nothingness.

This first struck me in a tangible way because my daughter, at the age of 3, had come unexpectedly to live in Ireland and I had rather belatedly to decide where we might send her to school. Being still of a fairly 'liberal' and 'pluralist' mindset, I found myself attracted by schools with a similar kind of ethos. But when I started to check them out, I was stuck by a paradox that seemed emblematic of something larger in my role and relationship with my child. The schools I investigated were all 'non-denominational', which I took to mean 'equally open to all beliefs'. I would have been happy for my daughter to receive a spiritual education that opened her up to God in a non-denominational sense. But, talking to the teachers and to other parents, it began to occur to me that, because we were in an overwhelmingly Catholic culture, 'non-denominational' meant not 'pluralist' but actually 'non-Catholic'. It became clear to me, for example, that, whereas many of the pupils would come, like my daughter, from a Catholic background, a minority would come from other faith backgrounds. Teasing out the nature of the religious curriculum, it dawned on me that the whole point of it was to teach Catholic children to be 'open' and 'tolerant' towards everyone else. But what, I wondered, would these children of wavering Catholic parents be taught for others to 'tolerate' in them? The answer was 'nothing'. They would be as the hole in the doughnut, surrounded by beliefs and traditions which they would be conditioned to tolerate, but themselves unburdened with anything to describe as beliefs of their own. The diversity of a culture depends on the individual vigour of its singularities. If you destroy the particularities which create the discrete entities of a culture, what is transmitted to the individual is not an interesting postmodern comprehension of paradoxical realities, but a sense that truth is a mirage.

The creation of just such confusion seems to me to be the inevitable outcome of what is termed the multicultural theory of postcolonial Ireland, which goes something like this: because we now have growing numbers of different faiths and traditions living among us, we cannot any longer imbue Catholic children with a sense that the Catholic religion is central or uniquely truthful. This sounds wonderfully tolerant, magnanimous and pluralist, until you consider what would happen if Catholics were to suggest to Muslims that they are not permitted to see Islam as central or uniquely truthful. If you are a Catholic, it is entirely natural to believe that Catholicism teaches the truth, and this in no way interferes with the right of others to believe the same of their own faith.

It is as though we are now expected to educate our children to the point of scepticism we ourselves have reached after several decades of intense struggle with the Catholic Church. Much of our thinking on these matters is what I term 'parasitic', which is to say that it rests on the assumption that everything we have come to know, understand and believe can be taken for granted, that it always existed and will remain in spite of all. This is a folly akin to sawing away the branch we are sitting on. Scepticism is the luxury of those who already have beliefs on which to exercise their doubts. But you cannot begin to comprehend the mysteries of existence from a position of doubt, only from having found your way on solid stepping stones to a place where you can pose the important questions. The transmission of beliefs requires to be informed by the concrete before it can afford to be infected by confusion.

Writing a few years ago on one of these controversies in the *Irish Times*, I asked: 'If my six-year-old child asks me a theological question, I do not burden her with the crypto-agnostic angst of my 47-year-old paradox-ridden head. When she asked, "Daddy, is heaven before or after outer space?" I did not tell her that heaven may be a product of man's inability to accept the nothingness of existence, which is what I might have said if I was being interviewed at the time by the religious correspondent of the *Irish Times*. Instead, I said, "After". And she said, "So, first you have the clouds, then you have the sky, then you have outer space, and then you have heaven. Right, Daddy?" And I said, "Right". Before you can learn to doubt, you must find something to have doubts about.'

I was beginning to understand something larger about the nature of faith and its inheritance. Before my daughter came along, to the extent that I thought about it at all, I would have imagined that I could bequeath a child of mine a sense of openness to the world which would enable her to arrive at her own answers to the big questions.

But faced with an actually existing child, it became clear to me that I had nothing to bequeath to her, and not just because I had lost my own way. I had broken away from the Church and obtained my freedom, and that, for me, amounted to a coherent, if fractured, spiritual journey. But I could not give her this. I could not give her my doubts, because these were inseparable from the certainties I had myself inherited. I could not give her my freedom, because it had dissolved into a new kind of imprisonment. Even if it had been intact, it would have been *my* freedom, and therefore non-transferable.

There is a paradox about faith and pluralism that secular liberals seem utterly incapable of perceiving. The notion of 'choice', which liberals are big on, is capable of bestowing benefits on only a single generation. It cannot be handed on. The present generation of neurotic Catholics, the Peter Pans who orchestrate the cultural conversation of modern Ireland on a day-to-day basis, are only capable of making a 'choice' about their religious practice (in most cases choosing not to practise) because they were handed a ready-made faith in the first place. Many of them think of themselves as atheists, agnostics or secular pluralists, but they are really lapsed Catholics whose worldview has been forged in the white heat of Catholicism. Their endless battling with the religion of their youth means that they have arrived at certain certainties, and may even have, to an extent, fulfilling spiritual lives. But post-Catholic neurosis, unlike Catholicism itself, cannot be handed on. It is reactive, and therefore incoherent, without knowledge of what it has rejected. It is consequently prone to sudden death, possibly after one, and certainly after two, generations. Faith, like culture, is not genetic: you cannot pass on a vacuum. The real test of liberal pluralism, therefore, is not the capacity to tolerate other people's beliefs but the capacity to tolerate in others the beliefs that you have rejected for yourself.

Perhaps the most intolerant phenomenon in present-day political culture is the notion of 'tolerance', which demands that everyone agree about everything, whether they like it or not. A 'wide-ranging tolerance and respect for all cultures and religions' results in the demolition of the singularity which is a prerequisite of both identity and belief. Pluralism is an admirable folly based on the spurious notion that religious bigotry and prejudice arise out of the differences between beliefs, when they invariably result from some previous misuses of power having set two tribes at each other's throats on the basis of a superficial apprehension of their more immediate differences.

In an effort to counter past or present intolerance, there is a strong strain in present Irish culture seeking to tolerate everything except that which is not 'other'. Those minorities who present themselves, believing what they may, are to be respected, tolerated, cherished and celebrated, but the majority get to believe in nothing except that everyone else is entitled to believe in what they choose. And what then do the children of the majority become but spectators at the carnival of belief which we have promoted, tolerated, affirmed, empowered, but declined to participate in? There is not much point in my being in favour of other people believing things if I do not believe in anything myself. Moreover, far from reassuring those with strong other beliefs, my lack of belief makes them uneasy and my supposed tolerance seems more like condescension. This will leave nothing but an empty shell looking benignly out on a teeming ferment of belief in which it has no part to play other than that of patronizing observer. In a sense, all religions are 'true'. What is important is that we leave open a functioning means of access to the truth, and the best way of ensuring this is to preserve the religion that surrounded us in childhood. To attack the particularity of that religion in the name of fostering 'pluralism' is akin to suppressing the English language out of 'respect' for Spanish and Italian.

The trouble with many discussions about the spiritual health of Ireland, then, is that they take place in a climate of prejudice or partisanship, which gives their language a tendentious hue. The voices raised are almost invariably those of either the triumphant proclaimers of a new, free and, by implication, godless Ireland, dancing on what they tell us is the grave of Irish Catholicism, or, in the opposite corner, the defenders of 'traditional' Catholicism repeating the mantras of a century ago. At most, these latter tend to convey the view that the loss of faith is a bad thing, in the sense of being immoral, that it will rebound badly on us, and that unbelievers are morally blameworthy for their unbelief. The trouble is that, since unbelievers do not feel bound by the morality that is invoked, such incantations tend towards tautology.

And because there is no sense of how our emerging secularism will adversely affect us in a practical sense, all this is unhelpful. I do not mean that it is unhelpful to Irish Catholicism's attempts to resuscitate itself, but rather that it is unhelpful to the general culture in achieving an understanding of what is happening and where the real danger lies.

It goes without saying that what sometimes seems to be the slow death of Irish Catholicism is more than an issue of institutional collapse. It is also a multifaceted cultural phenomenon, affecting society in the most profound way. I suspect we do not yet have even the faintest sense of the long-term implications.

When we allow the possibility of negative consequences at all, we talk vaguely about social breakdown, hedonism, loss of 'moral' fibre and so forth. But there is a far more fundamental danger in the loss of faith: the destruction of the motor of human existence as we have taken it for granted over many centuries. No matter what the rationality of secularism, societies simply do not survive long without having within them some critical mass of religious believers. God and hope can not long be separated.

# — 7 —

# The Great Hunger

For a lengthy and intense period after the difficulties over my daughter, I became obsessed with clothes. I still don't quite know why. Until then I had had not the slightest interest, other than to have a spare sports jacket, a clean shirt and maybe a suit for weddings and funerals. For years I only ever had one pair of shoes at a time. During my Yosser period, things got much worse because I was spending all my money on air tickets and lawyers. I don't recall during that period ever once caring about what I wore or how I looked. I bought no clothes at all, and shoes or boots only when I absolutely needed to. Then, when the nightmare ended, I observed myself changing. I remember, after a year of sheer terror, having actual free time to do something or nothing, as I pleased – being able to go out for a walk one spring evening and feeling the exhilaration of seeing, hearing and smelling again as though for the first time. Then one day I went into a shop and bought myself a shirt. It wasn't an expensive shirt, nor even a particularly flamboyant one, but buying it seemed to express some-thing about the change for the better that my life was beginning to manifest. I brought it home and put it in my wardrobe. The next day I bought another one. Then I bought a suit. I never wore suits, hated them actually, but since everything else about me had been changed by the experience I'd just been through, I thought maybe I'd give it a try. My left-leaning disposition had been collapsed by the sense of abandonment I'd felt during the difficulties and I thought that maybe a suit, after all, might be the very thing. Then I bought another suit. Then I started to visit charity shops and delighted in finding items that were cheap but new. I bought several more shirts and suits and stashed them in the wardrobe with the others. I didn't wear any of them. If you'd asked me why, I'd have said that I had nowhere particular to go, but that wouldn't have been the case. I was going places all the time, but in retrospect I recognize that each day I would weigh up the possibility of wearing one of my new shirts or suits and nearly always decide against it. No, I would think wordlessly to myself, today is not a day that merits a new shirt – this old one will do.

I began to watch myself more carefully. My store of shirts and suits and sports jackets started to grow, at first steadily and then, it seemed, exponentially. To be completely truthful, it is still growing. I could take a look to see how many unopened shirts, unworn suits and still pristine sports jackets I now have, but I am too ashamed to look too closely. When occasionally I decide that a particular day or night is worth the investment of one of my new shirts, I rummage with one eye, avoiding the quantum of thread and focusing on the particular.

Do I know what it's about? I have my theories. One theory is that I am waiting for my life to begin. I have a plan for my life, perhaps not fully formulated, and certainly not articulated, but a plan nonetheless. I seem to think there is a point somewhere up ahead, perhaps in a week or a month or at most a year, when things will all of a sudden get better in a sort of permanent way. This doesn't necessarily mean that things are bad as they are, but simply that they are not good enough. There is an imperfection in reality that bothers me, or at least renders me unable to participate in a wholehearted way, for the moment anyway, which seems to amount to longer than I intended. As time moves on, the shirts became more colourful, often belonging to a version of me that fails to accord with any previous version, as though I am planning not one but several full lives.

I do something similar with books. I buy books all the time, because they interest me or excite me or because everyone is talking about them. I take them home and put them on a shelf with all the other books I've bought for the same reasons. I read some of them, it is true, but rather fewer than the number I don't read. I'm keeping them, I think, for some amorphous era up ahead when my life will be more conducive to reading, perhaps when I retire, or move to the country. Yes, I rather fancy the idea of reading books all day in coffee shops near the harbour of a town somewhere westish. When people visit me at home they survey my shelves and ask, nearly always, 'Have you read them all?' I say, 'Not all', which is a kind of lie because it implies that there may be one or two that I haven't (yet) read. In my heart I know that the reading project is pretty hopeless, that if I were to read all the books I've bought to date, I would need to retire straight away and live to a hundred and five. And I'm still buying books as if there was, as it were, no tomorrow. Sometimes I tell myself that I should stop buying books until I've read all the ones I have, but these phases don't last long. I usually get myself going again by convincing myself that, even if I don't get to read them all, I can leave them for my daughter. But then I think, 'What if she's just like me?' And after that I think, 'What if she's not at all like me and puts them all in a skip?'

It all brings me back to my father. As I wrote in my first book, *Jiving at the Crossroads*, my father collected things. He had a shopful of tools in the front room of our house, and still bought a new tool practically every time he needed one. Each tool would be used perhaps once or twice, and then mummified in newspaper to keep it from rusting. When he needed such a tool again, he would buy a new one, perhaps because he had forgotten what was in the individual parcels laid out on shelves in his 'shop' or because he did not want to disturb one of the tools he already had for a minor matter such as fixing a tap washer or hanging a picture. He wasn't much of a man for clothes, but he had a good suit which he never wore. Most of the time he dressed in rags. I watch myself sometimes and, recognizing him in my behaviour, wonder if he watched himself and wondered where his behaviour came from. I can't imagine that he didn't.

I used to put it down to the Famine, otherwise known as 'The Great Hunger', that hit Ireland in the mid-nineteenth century, when my father's grandparents would have been in their middle years. I assume the mark it left got handed on somehow. I still think there might be something in this, but no longer believe it's the full story. I used to think of my father as someone who was simply into storing things up as a safeguard against future want, as though this idea had been implanted upon him by received experience. Because he was much older than most other children's fathers, he seemed to come from deeper into history and to carry its wounds more visibly. But I no longer think this is what it was. I believe this was a superficial apprehension of something far more interesting. If my father's storing up of tools was an expression of some deep fear of deprivation, it was at a symbolic rather than a literal level, for in everything else he was the most unmaterialistic of human beings.

There is in Ireland a particular and superficially peculiar use of the word 'want' to signify some deep-seated need or longing. Usually you hear it used in relation to someone who has erupted into public notice, perhaps posthumously, on account of some unanticipated act of violence towards himself or others. 'He had a want in him,' they say, by way of beginning the process of finding an explanation. But perhaps we all have 'wants' in us.

What do we mean when we say, as we do in Ireland all the time now, that shopping is 'the new religion'? In one sense, the answer is obvious: we have replaced the zeal we once displayed for godliness with a fanaticism for materialism. Or, you might note that the weekend, once our time of repose and spiritual reflection, is nowadays the eye of the consumerist maelstrom. Or, that the spaces in which we nowadays shop (and it is much more a verb now than it was) resemble greatly places of what we used to call 'worship'. The new shopping malls, which sprout in today's Ireland like daffodils, seem, accidentally or otherwise, to feel, from the inside, like cathedrals, pointing skywards but with escalators criss-crossing in mid-ascent, as though to create a sense of normality around the idea of assumption.

In the past decade, Irish society has been transmogrified by money, and that change has many manifestations. But the most obvious, immediate, visible, public change is in the way we shop, the way we perceive the act of shopping, the meaning we attribute to the things we buy. Once we bought things because we needed them: the makings of a meal, a new shirt, a suit, a pair of winter boots. Usually, this meant a dedicated trip to a particular shop, or perhaps 'the shops'. We still perhaps do these things, but they have blurred into an entirely different function, which on the surface has the appearance of shopping for shopping's sake. If you visit a large shopping centre at any time during an average weekday, you will find it is full of people. No, let us be precise, it will be three-quarters full of women, with the minority of men either providing plastic back-up or there alone on a mission which still resembles the traditional act of shopping. This is the most obvious but rarely articulated particularity of the new culture of shopping: it is mainly driven by women. A man out shopping is still usually looking for a pair of socks or a new suit; a woman is looking for herself. I believe this has something to do with women's daily involvement with children. I say this because I seem, perhaps unusually for a man, to have experienced something like it myself since my daughter came along, as thought the exploration of materialism is a way of finding yourself again, of rescuing yourself from the blurring of identity that comes from close daily involvement with children. This is my latest excuse for all those shirts.

This line of speculation has many interesting resonances, but in the context of shopping-as-quasi-religion, it has a rather fascinating subtext. In Ireland, as in most European cultures, women were traditionally the driving force of the family's religious life and observance. It was women who policed in the home the moral prescriptions of the Catholic Church, and maintained the more implacable visage of piety in the face of male scepticism, anti-clericalism or dissent. Nowadays it is women who lead their men into the new temples of Mammon. This is more than a moral observation, and may not be that at all. Something happens in the core of the human being to shift her or him from the spiritual to the material plane. It is not simply that she stops believing in God, or that he is waylaid by the opportunities offered by money. We need to state the case more precisely. What happens is that the individual's understanding of the prospect of his or her own chances of happiness has altered profoundly. We have moved from a culture in which the idea of happiness was bound up with the next life, to one in which the idea of happiness has boomeranged and begun to hover around ourselves. We have pulled back our horizons from the distance beyond which we cannot imagine and laid them down within ourselves.

Almost all the outlets in a typical modern shopping centre are nowadays dedicated to raiment, accessory or grooming. There are still the food stores and the furniture shops, but mainly it is clothes and other items or services whose purpose is the presentation of the individual to the outside world. This, too, has traditionally been a female preoccupation: until recently, men's sense of how they looked was defined by ethics of understatement and conformity, though this is changing. What we are being offered in the boutique or shoe shop is the opportunity or, if you prefer, the illusion of happiness based on the way we see ourselves in our most idealized physical form. We go to the shopping centre with a variety of fantasies sketched in the backs of our minds, and there, with the help of advertising, pampering and flattery, we emerge each time with what we imagine to be the makings of a new self. A pair of jeans is no longer something to wear, but part of a technology of being, with the label having more importance than the material which covers us up. Among the many pratfalls of this doomed procedure resides the absurdity that the constant re-creation of this new self involves outlays of increasingly large sums of money in return for a constantly reducing sense of satisfaction. The faster we veer off into the materialist domain in search of ourselves, the faster our human identity dissolves. And as our authentic sense of self diminishes, we require more and more of what is termed 'exclusivity' in order to define ourselves anew.

It seems to me there's no point in being sanctimonious about this. We come from a great want. There is a tendency nowadays in Ireland for us to lecture one another, to bemoan our decline into material hedonism, to lament the collapse of spiritual values, whatever they were. 'Spirituality' is the new buzzword that people use to differentiate their beliefs from Catholicism, but nobody seems sure what it means. It has for some time seemed to me that it might be a good idea for us to scrap the word 'spirituality' and talk about something more easily comprehensible, perhaps happiness or ease or freedom. Perhaps if we really began to look at it, we'd come to realize that all that's changed is the focus of our searching. It seems to me pointless telling people that they should turn away from materialism and back to spirituality. You might as well have told those people clambering over the remains of the Berlin Wall in 1989 that they should turn back and rebuild it because they wouldn't find what they were looking for in the materialist West. As with the mantra about lost 'morality', I sometimes think it might be a good idea to suspend all this talk about a loss of 'spiritual values'. Instead, and in the absence of judgementalism, perhaps we should simply observe ourselves and how we behave and ask what exactly we are looking for.

I already have enough shirts in my wardrobe, but when I see another shirt that I like, something happens to me. Some unregistered kind of fantasy begins to kick in, telling me that this is the shirt that will make a real difference, the one that will make me happy, make the woman of my dreams fall in love with me on the spot. The one that will make me whole. I can't buy it at first. Maybe we carry this guilt from the Famine and before, a sense that indulging ourselves is some kind of sin for which a penalty will be exacted. So I walk away, maybe even leave. But I come back later with my rationalizations. There is something deeply satisfying, dare I say intoxicating, about buying something you want – or think you want. Perhaps the guilt makes the climax even more exhilarating. Perhaps two kinds of endorphins surge through the arteries and converge in a kind of endorphin gridlock that makes me dizzy with longing and shame. I have no difficulty believing that there is indeed some deep physical call that is answered by the process of shopping for things that are not outright necessities. And so I return in the end, having quieted my conscience. And then in a series of practised moves, I buy the shirt and bring it home. I don't take it out of the bag, but stash it with the others and maybe then forget about it. There is this law-of-diminishing-returns effect that seems to dog these attempts at fantasy-fulfilment: the shirt which, on the hanger in the shop, looked like the one I'd been searching for all my life, seems to lose its magic once I've brought it home. I leave it in its bag and throw it in the wardrobe, and then, a week or two later I come across it, and take it out. But it's never the same shirt. Or at least it never has quite the same capacity to summon up the fantasy it did at the moment of intoxication. Its happiness potential has evaporated in the wardrobe and I am returned to my searching.

With cars, the stakes are higher. A few years ago, a retired senior Catholic cleric delivered a caustic judgment on changing Irish mores. 'It is puerile', said the retired Cardinal Cahal Daly, 'to buy symbols such as a four-wheel drive and to think that owning these things can give you status.' He had a point. There is undoubtedly something silly about a culture in which the kind of car you drive has become such a powerful indicator of who or what you are. But the Cardinal's choice of word – 'puerile' – suggests that he finds the modern preoccupation with motor vehicles an immature or childish phenomenon, and in truth it is much sillier than that.

I was reminded of my late friend and journalist colleague John

Healy's rationalization for buying himself a Rolls Royce for the sole purpose of driving it – just once – into his home town, Charlestown. He, too, recognized the gesture as silly, but, as he put it, 'If that is the measurement of achievement in the society, then yes, there it is, I have it.' He sold the car quietly after a short time. One of the most profound changes of the past couple of decades has been the shift in the way Irish society dispenses esteem, the languages it offers us to express our sense of self-worth. In my boyhood, I saw my father dressed in rags being valued by society to the status of a cardinal because he worked hard and treated people with gentleness. But such mediums of esteem are no longer regarded as viable currencies. To say that our language of mutual estimation has shifted from the moral to the material is not to make a moral statement, but merely to note the facts. We now seek to buy what once we had to earn. You could moralize about that, but I don't see the point: both approaches are based on error and behind both is the same yearning. What we are going through now, the relentless pursuit of the material, reveals itself as much more than it appears, and perhaps ultimately as a searching for love.

The point is that we do not, as individuals, choose the symbols with which we must declare ourselves, nor can we control the meanings they generate if we cease to pay them proper attention. There is nothing childish about the symbolism of motor vehicles. The meanings relate completely to the adult world, and there not merely to status, but to personality, sexuality, even identity itself.

You might well argue that this indicates a spiritual collapse – which I believe was close to the Cardinal's point. But we need to look deeper, to the way Irish society has changed from a social hierarchy in which everyone was accorded a ranking on the basis of respectability and piety, to one in which money is the measure of everything. As a child, one of the most pathos-saturated scenes I witnessed was the sight of the elderly parents of a successful local blade being dropped at the church gates in the new car. To see a pinched and self-conscious couple scrambling shamefacedly from a dazzling spaceship of a Sunbeam Rapier was to see the effects of the hierarchy bearing down on the generations, withholding permission to step beyond your ranking. Nowadays the church car park is a battle of the chariots.

Throughout most of my adulthood, I would have agreed with the

Cardinal. But then I saw the Alfa Romeo 156 T-spark, and fell in love, and my view of four-wheeled life has not been the same since. The idea that, as an *Irish Times* columnist, I did not necessarily have to drive an ugly car was akin to my first discovery of sex or alcohol.

'Oh right!' you say. 'A mid-life crisis – how novel and interesting!' But no: I have simply arrived at that point reached by Patrick Kavanagh on the canal bank: the point of not caring. Except that, this being a half-century on, my indifference is directed against neither the sackcloth-and-ashes of traditional piety, nor the vulgarity of new money in what we call 'modern' Ireland, but against the high priests of the Peter Pan establishment, who mix and match their tyrannics with the time of day.

The Cardinal may well have been talking about me. That very year, I had bought myself an Alfa GT. I couldn't resist it, for it seemed the most beautiful car that ever nosed onto a public road. I was not without guilt, but on balance it was a good experience. Perhaps Cardinal Daly was right: perhaps it is puerile. But it is a long time since I felt so good with my clothes on. I may as well come completely clean while I'm at it: I also have a pair of Alfa Romeo cufflinks. I caught sight of them in a display in the showroom and wouldn't leave until the salesman had found the key to the glass case and gave them to me. I wear them sometimes, but not often. I'm keeping them for a special occasion. Sometimes, when I do wear them, people who have known me for some time, but not particularly intimately, look at me in a new way, or even say something – an expression of their shock, even disappointment. They wouldn't have put me down for a cufflinks kind of guy, never mind an Alfa Romeo cufflinks kind of guy. Sometimes I am quite relieved my father is no longer around.

As a youngster, I adored cars. My father had in his youth trained as a mechanic and had godlike powers over engines. A man once described to me seeing him fix a broken driveshaft by using the branch of a tree as a splint. The van shuddered to a halt on a country road between Ballinagare and Elphin. He got out for a look underneath and then delivered his verdict: broken driveshaft. Immediately he set off across the ditch towards a small wood. He was gone for about ten minutes and returned with a length of timber and a hoop of barbed wire. He recruited his passenger as assistant and got back under the vehicle. The passenger fed through, on demand, the tools from the box behind the driver's seat, and after a quarter of an hour or so, my father emerged, having repaired the broken driveshaft with an improvised splint. He started up and drove gingerly home.

I didn't inherit much of the mechanical bent, but I knew what I liked. In a hazy period in the 1970s, I owned an MG Midget, an MGBGT and a Triumph Spitfire, of which the Midget, pet-named Brigid, was the love of my life. Then, for more than twenty years, politics took over. My head could no longer be turned by a pair of shapely wing-sections. I declined into what I now describe as my 'PC phase', in which the functionality of the car became not just more important than looks, but precisely the statement I wanted my car to make about me. I drove a Fiesta, a Toyata Tercel, two Clios and three different versions of the same yawn-inducing Rover. I have a sense that this phase coincided with a period in which the Western motor mainstream succumbed to ugliness of an almost masochistic kind. In the 1980s, aesthetics became not merely secondary but almost irrelevant. I blame the Japanese. Back in the 1960s and 1970s, although there were certainly some pig-ugly cars on the road, there were also some beautiful Rovers, Mercs, Wolsleys, as well as classics such as the Mini and VW Beetle. The problem that developed thereafter arose from the mechanical unreliability we had taken for granted. In those days, you really didn't expect your car to start every day. Two out of three was pretty good, especially in winter, and it was by no means an embarrassment to have to ask for a shove. But then the Japanese arrived with their Datsuns and Toyotas, and put an end to all that. Their arrival coincided with the fading of the sixties dream, the dropping hemline and 4-4-2 football. After that, your car might be rusting to death, but it would always start. And with this reliability came a phlegmatic contempt for form, which rapidly spread to the European manufacturers. Thus began the era of the functional Ford, the Cortina, the Corsair, the Fiesta, a range of breezeblock Fiats and the occasional fruity Opel.

Cars then became a kind of anti-statement, an avoidance of beauty, a reflection of the dour, recessionary times. To drive a beautiful car was to reveal yourself as a frivolous person, unaware of the seriousness of the general situation. Even if you'd picked it up for next to nothing at an auction, you had to spend so much time explaining how you'd got it – by way of apologizing for having it – that the fun was knocked out of it. To blend in was to drive an invisible car – a Hillman Hunter, perhaps, or an Opel Kadett. For myself, I drove nondescript cars for the same reason I wore woolly jumpers: to avoid anything that might indicate acquiescence in the corporate mainstream. Fiestas and Clios, let's face it, were girls' cars. For a woman they represented acquiescence in the concept of the 'little woman'; for a man to drive one went far beyond a loudly professed fondness for something 'nippy about town' – it was a safety valve for his existential guilt, a disavowal of the big-mickey motor, an asexual statement of brotherly solidarity in the sisterly cause, an acceptance of the Naomi Wolf idea that beauty is a spurious aesthetic designed to perpetuate the patriarchy. 'Trust me, Sisters,' it screeched, 'I am in touch with my fuel-consumption.' Buying an Alfa Romeo, like wearing a suit, was a kind of perverse diametricism, a way of reminding myself that I no longer subscribed to a form of self-effacement that might, in truth, be doing me in.

And this is where Cardinal Daly's observation revealed to me its fault lines. He was, as I wrote at the time, mistaken in believing that a new phenomenon had manifested itself as a result of the Celtic Tiger. 'I can see what the Cardinal is getting at,' I wrote in of all places the motoring section of the *Irish Times*, 'but I don't believe I'll go to hell because I didn't drive a Daewoo.' For in truth the statement represented by a Fiesta or a Clio was at least as puerile as that made by a Merc or a BMW. All that had happened was that the symbols had changed because we'd become more honest, something any cleric must surely applaud.

Of course, the motor fantasy is at least as subject to the law of diminishing returns as the shirt or the suit fantasy. Twice in my life I've bought new cars and had them scratched in the first week. Immediately, the object of my dreams was turned into a massive scratch on wheels, its magic depleted and its gilt turned to guilt. For as long as the dream remains intact, the guilt seems to stay – relatively – at bay. At least, I reassure myself, I'm living life to the full. But then, when the realization dawns that this object, garment or accessory is not after all going to change me radically, all I am left with are the payments and the sense of having been fooled by myself.

This is the materialist trap: the promise of something that isn't, in truth, possible. Even when these things in themselves do make us happy, if only for a while, our sense of nirvana is entirely in our own heads. The idea, on which our fantasy is predicated, that other people see us in accordance with our own self-image is entirely bogus. When I leave the showroom and drive somewhat shamefacedly home, what others see, if they see anything at all – is a middle-aged man in a rather ostentatious car, wearing a pink shirt that looks kind of new. They don't see the fantasy, or at most they see a shadow of it. And when this dawns on me, as occasionally it does, I wish for my old car back. I want to put all those shirts in a black bin-liner and deliver them to Oxfam. But something prevents me, and it isn't as simple as meanness. I believe it's because these shirts, however ridiculous, are the symbols of something vital, something central to my nature, something utterly real.

Consumerism is a simple enough theory – it equates personal happiness with the purchase of material possessions. So can a new shirt make me happy? Actually, it can, up to a point. I get a buzz from it, from the promise of the fantasy and sometimes from the enjoyment of the thing itself, though this is never as great as the promise. Consumerism breaks its promises: the payments start, the credit card bills arrive, and there's nothing to show for it, nothing to feel for it, except the oddly nondescript garment offering more questions than answers. The real problem about retail therapy is not a moral one, but has to do with the more mundane matter of credit card statements and the guilt that tends to precede, accompany and escalate from the process of trying to define myself in this way. In theory, the credit card is supposed to delay the moment of reckoning, by a month, or, if you're clever, almost two. But anyone who has ever used one unwisely will know that, in reality, the guilt begins from the moment the assistant swipes your card on that machine that never seems to forget or make a mistake. There is a hangover from consumption as real as the one you get from alcohol: the return of the repressed guilt multiplied by the figure at the end of the bank statement. In a sense, buying stuff has the same effect in our lives as booze or drugs – instant gratification followed by a disquieting queasiness. But the intellectual knowledge of either this outcome or the intrinsic futility of the process seems not to penetrate the condition, which constantly seeks opportunities to repeat itself.

As they learn in the first module at marketing school, selling is fundamentally about fantasy: the project of constructing our future selves is a constant work-in-progress, and it is the function of advertising to keep us reminded of this. I see, through a showroom window, a car that I think will make me whole, or at least more whole than I am now. On my less insecure days, a shirt will meet the same need. Irish culture today is split on the question of aggressive exploitation or sanctimonious contempt. In between, the individual is left bereft of explanation other than one that makes him feel guilty. The crude moral conversation we tend to have about materialism is wont to tell me that this urge to buy things is evidence of my spiritual under-development. Perhaps it is, but then I don't have any difficulty in acknowledging that my spiritual growth is a work-in-progress. In any event, I really don't believe that wearing an old shirt or driving an old banger of itself makes me a more spiritual person. Such notions, surely, are part of the misapprehensions from which we are retreating.

We are material as well as spiritual beings and the celebration of life is a primary spiritual function. I have frequently acknowledged to myself the paradox that, by wearing old clothes when my wardrobe is full of new ones, I may – far from displaying some ascetic sanctimony – be flinging God's bounty back in His face. I don't mean the shirts, so much as the day, the unique and beautiful day in which I am breathing now, and which, for no reason that I can quite get my head around, I don't quite seem to value as much as some other day not yet dawned and somehow receding before me over the horizon of time. It's as though I'm not quite ready. Preparing, yes. Anticipating, yes. Enthusiastic even. But yet, like a suspicious shopkeeper holding a tenner up to the light, I scrutinize each new dawn for signs that it will be The One, and then write it off before it starts.

Perhaps the urge to buy clothes or cars is not driven primarily by a simple desire to look good or even to make us attractive to others. Perhaps it is a convoluted expression of something else. In *The Religious Sense*, Father Luigi Giussani writes about how we carry within us an imprint of heavenly perfection and search in this world for its echo. It is as though we go around the world searching for the lock into which the key we were born with will fit and turn. But all the locks seem wrong.

The 'new religion', then, would be aptly named because it is, fundamentally, about the attempted transformation of each one of us into a goddess or god, an endeavour doomed to failure. But perhaps what is most interesting about this is that the urge, the desire, is so strong. Perhaps, rather than bemoaning this, we should take comfort from it, because it may bespeak the health of a deeper yearning. What are we searching for among all these trinkets and baubles? It's easy to decide that it's mere self-indulgence, vulgarity: what my father used to call conceit. But what if it's more? What if what we're searching for is something we cannot do without? What if what we're pursuing is the very stuff of heaven itself?

It's as if all these explorations of the material are like illicit affairs with false ideas of myself. Each time I embark upon one with a light heart which surges with hope, excitement and expectation, and each time it ends in a squalid familiarity of recrimination, fear and guilt. No matter how often I traverse the same road, I seem not to recognize it or remember where it leads. Something drives me on and it isn't anything as prosaic as lust. I am driven by a dream I don't remember having. Each time, when the collapse begins to gather itself, I flounder around in search of reasons: first why it's not working and can perhaps be put right, then why it's not working and isn't my fault, then why it's not working and why it couldn't have been foreseen. It never seems to be admissible that the enterprise was doomed from the start, that it had a shape which is the same shape as other attempts to find myself where, if I paused to think about it, there was never any prospect of finding anything but disappointment. This enterprise has a shape, which never changes: it goes up and then it comes down. It is, when I stand back and look at it, a pointy thing going up to the sky and then returning rapidly to earth, a bit like myself, but not enough like myself to convince me.

One September morning a couple of years ago, I was out walking near my home along the unmarked border between Dalkey and Killiney in south County Dublin. As I was approaching the footbridge to White Rock beach in Killiney, I encountered a man on the path ahead of me trying to attract my attention. I was at that moment listening to an economic discussion on my Walkman and was not in the mood for conversation. With some irritation I removed my earphones. Nobody was drowning: the man simply wanted to remark on the gloriousness of the morning and the beauty of the place. He waved his arm across the horizon, taking in the sweep of the bay from Dalkey Island to Bray Head, the low-tide serenity of the seascape veiled in a thin heat haze. 'Look at it!' he said. 'You wouldn't know whether to eat it or drink it or ride it. But I have to go to work now. If only there was some kind of a pause button you could press and then come back later.' Then he walked away back to his car.

His words stayed in my head for most of the day. The frustration he had so eloquently articulated goes deeper than having to work on a sunny day. I feel it myself a lot of the time. 'So what?' you say. 'It's part of the human condition.' But it seems conspicuously to be a part of the human condition in Ireland, and more so now than ever. The man was saying, for himself and for me, that we have been caught in a trap. Peace, freedom and happiness, which we go about the place searching for in baubles and diversions, are much of the time right there in front of our noses, but, going around in circles trying to find them elsewhere – on a shelf, in a mirror or in someone else's eyes – we miss them and walk past.

The modern economy is good at getting us to postpone our lives little by little in the expectation that, sometime, maybe soon, we will be able to let go and enjoy the world in a free and unbounded way. Money is the technology we use for achieving this postponement: it stores up our credits and deep-freezes our hopes until the time comes when we can permit ourselves to live. We turn our backs on the present so we can focus on accumulation, projecting forward to Christmas, summer holidays, retirement, but all the time with this gnawing sense that we could be living right now for next to nothing, if only we could see things half straight. This is a condition burned into the souls of the Irish people by a history of want.

The feeling I think we have is of being part of a machine, a machine that grinds mercilessly week after week, demanding of us that we put our lives on hold, dump our children in the crèche, mortgage ourselves to the hairline and run ever faster to stand still on the M50. We want to stop and get off, but the moment never seems to be right. The machine trundles on and we live in fear that if we lose our footing it will grind us between its wheels. It bullies us with pace and bribes us with promises to persuade us that, if we keep faith with it, it will take us to the Promised Land. And all the time, even as we grow wearier and angrier, the promises become louder and louder, so that, though dispirited and exhausted, we consent to go on once again. But more and more the feeling grows that we are going nowhere rather than somewhere, that we live in a land where the miracle of the loaves and fishes has been put into reverse, and that the more we pedal the less we achieve.

I propose we stop talking about spirituality and 'the spiritual vacuum' and begin talking about materialism: what it really is, what it really does. We are both spiritual and material beings and it's unhealthy to get out of balance. Too much spirituality is as bad as too little. We have to live here too, not in the clouds.

Without the prospect of happiness we are dead. When hope dies, we kill ourselves, one way or another, and whether we do it with drink or knives hardly matters much in the end. Human beings who are not happy, or who do not have at least the hope of happiness, will not get out of bed in the morning. If you leave God out of it for a moment, life is going nowhere rather than somewhere. You can wear only one shirt in the grave.

A good few years ago, while researching some articles about the growing trend of suicide in Ireland, I met a man called Bartley Sheehan, who was a GP in Dun Laoghaire as well as the local county coroner. We were talking about suicide. I asked him, 'Dr Sheehan, why do people kill themselves?' He paused before answering. 'That's not the right question,' he said. 'The question is why we *don't* all kill ourselves.'

There are reason we don't kill ourselves, reasons we get up in the morning and live our lives. Some people find it in the love of their families. Others in art and creativity. Others fix their gazes on the next world. But for the great mass of people, pummelled by a world inhospitable to love, the search for happiness is more and more focused on lifestyle, status and possessions. Love, art, money, sex, drugs, God – these are the things that keep us alive. In this contest, if you boil off the natural tendency towards judgementalism, they are the life-giving qualities, neither good nor bad. But without at least one of them we will lose the will to live. And of these, only two endure: God and love. And in a very real sense these are not two, but One. This is not something we can simply be told. We need to find it out for ourselves, sometimes more than once. We need to examine the options, take their measure, take them for test drives, try them out, try them on.

Every second day the Irish newspapers carry a story relating to a symptom of what seems like some kind of collective unease, if not psychic disintegration, of the Irish people. Consulting the morning newspapers as I was writing this, I instantly located two: a report of a study indicating that we're now putting on weight faster than most of our European neighbours (the weight of an average citizen has over the past four years increased by 1.6 kgs/3.5 lbs), and a story about Irish people having more frequent thoughts about suicide than any other nationality. Whatever you make of these stories in themselves, what they say about us more generally is that we have lately started to become alert to changes in our psychic make-up in a manner that would have seemed comical to previous generations.

In parallel with the growth of this psychic hypochondria, there has developed a new industry in pseudo-therapeutic analysis, usually manifesting at conferences in which various 'experts' expostulate about what it all means. What most of these over-reported exercises in self-analysis have in common is their avoidance of hard, and therefore potentially controversial, questions concerning social, political or religious realities. There is much talk about happiness, about obesity and binge-drinking, about the decline in spiritual values arising from consumerism. But in what sense are we unhappy? How does eating and drinking to excess arise from unhappiness? What, indeed, is unhappiness? What is consumerism? What does the word 'spiritual' actually mean and can it be divorced from the idea of God? The denouncement of 'consumerism' is one of the blossoming by-products of Ireland's recent successes, even as, laden with carrier bags in the shopping centre, we strain to escape from each other's company for fear that we might go home with loose change burning holes in our pockets. It is part of a more widespread and seemingly inevitable strain of hypocrisy in our society, which seeks to deny by disparagement the truth of how we live, as though to distance our individual selves from the general culture, implying that, 'of course, I only behave like this because I am trapped in a form of society that appals me' (even as it maintains me in the comfort to which I have become accustomed!).

This tendency, I believe, is born of a largely unremarked disjunction in societal thinking, which nurtures a spurious division between the material and what is called the 'spiritual'. This split appears especially pronounced in present-day Christian thinking, which seems to experience great difficulty in reconciling with itself mankind's necessary attachment to things of the flesh.

The recent alteration in Ireland's circumstances has been the source of more generalized, but as yet unreported, reflection and soul searching. Whereas on the one hand, people simply get on with enjoying the new circumstances, on the other there has developed a strand of self-accusation and unhappiness with the very idea of prosperity, which in some ways does not suit the Irish temperament. A couple of years ago, I wrote about a speech made by President Mary McAleese at a conference in County Clare, in which she warned of Irish society entering a 'cul-de-sac of complacent consumerism'. We are facing, she argued, a choice between becoming an egalitarian, compassionate Republic or a society 'wrapped in individualism', deaf to 'the voices of the excluded'. We must learn, she said, to 'carry our shopping bags in one hand and our consciences in the other'. President McAleese is an extremely thoughtful woman whose background is in intellectual Catholicism. Her remarks were reasonably typical of the tone and content of analysis from a Christian perspective of the drift of Irish society since the arrival of the Celtic Tiger in the 1990s. And, bizarrely, it was typical, not merely of how the issue had come to be represented in church circles and by church people but also of a certain strand in public commentary from left-wing, secular sources. The former approach the matter from the perspective of a literal application of the Christian message, whereas the latter seek to condemn the ethical content of Christianity by pointing up its failure in the face of the growing inequality in Irish society. I have chiefly in mind not any coherent left-wing philosophy, which simply does not exist in Ireland, but rather the influence of a woolly left-wing thinking adopted as a badge of identity and moral superiority by certain elements of the

Peter Pan establishment, and still not shaken off, regardless of world events or personal circumstances. Many such people now occupy positions in political organizations and the media, or in other situations where their ideas remain unaffected by their own growing prosperity. Because crude left-wing rhetoric has become unfashionable, many of their pronouncements are couched less in the jargon of Marxism than, bizarrely, in the prescriptions of Christianity. It is often they, rather than priests and bishops, who remind us of our duty to the poor, of Christ's injunction to love our neighbour. But in purportedly demonstrating that a Christian society is in breach of its own principles, what the left-liberal is precisely demanding is that Christians live by their own ideals or cease articulating them. He would invariably prefer the latter outcome. Suspecting, however, that his demands are unlikely to be met, he settles for the warm glow arising from the felt moral superiority of his position.

Writing about the President's speech in a Catholic magazine, *The Voice Today*, I admitted that I frequently found myself saying similar things. Most of us wrestle with these questions all the time, torn between self-indulgence, guilt and occasional bouts of charity. How do we meet Christ's injunction to love our neighbour and give to the poor? In order to be truly Christian, must we ourselves become poor? How, in a world where want and grief continue to rage through the lives of so many, can we, who enjoy such seemingly undeserved stability and prosperity, reconcile our good fortune with the Christian challenge to love our neighbour? Is it possible to be Christian and rich? If not, how poor does one have to become? Is it sufficient to give a little more than the average alms-giver and accuse society generally of not being as Christian as you are? Or perhaps it is enough, as many clerics seem to believe, to denounce the system of economics by which our society lives.

We get little help with this dilemma from our spiritual leaders. Their recipe is generally rather bland – mild injunctions concerning Christian charity, occasional hectoring about gratitude, but with no real clarity or conviction. It often seems to me that the Christian message, as presented in modern societies, achieves little other than the multiplication of guilt, which has the effect of turning people away, not from consumerism, but from Christianity.

The reason for the evasion is obvious: Christian clerics, too, are caught in the conundrum; they too live in the fortunate zone. All their sermons achieve is an increase in the store of collective guilt, without gain for those deemed to be 'less fortunate'.

This woolliness has, I believe, caused much damage to Christianity, though not for the reasons usually inferred. In general, when we think about the problem at a conscious level, we tend to flagellate ourselves a little and then go on as before. We accuse ourselves of, for example, insufficient generosity to the poor, or perhaps of hypocrisy on account of our continuing to espouse values we fall far short of living up to. But our self-accusation is short lived, because, even if any of us is personally inclined to act by what we understand as Christian principles, there seems to be very little that, acting independently, any one of us can achieve in tackling the enormity of global pain and inequality. The process begins with a kind of privatization of the Christian message, followed by a suppression of its sting, followed by a degree of personal disquiet in the heart of the individual Christian, followed by a slight turning away from that message by virtue of its accusation.

And this turning away causes us to embrace Mammon with ever greater conviction, as if only by selfishness can we achieve the kind of clarity we crave. It is not so much that money and the baubles of the marketplace themselves turn our heads, as that, unable to reconcile our own prosperity with what we have internalized of Christ's message, and unable to relinquish our comfort and wealth, we tend to postpone grappling with the matter and lapse into a further withdrawal from the message. At the end of the process, we turn a little farther away from Jesus Christ, not because we resent Him, but because, unable to live up to his injunctions and, perhaps having quieted the voice of conscience by a self-serving rationalization, we decide that we may as well be hung for sheep as for lambs.

I sense that we in Western societies are becoming increasingly successful at quieting our consciences, and not entirely for blameworthy reasons. The atheist Sigmund Freud, in *Civilization and its Discontents*, argued in effect that we are already overburdened with conscience. The cultural superego, which is carried in cultural ethics and social norms, has imposed upon us such a level of socially necessary guilt that individual happiness is impossible. Conscience, he wrote, 'troubles too little about the happiness of the ego, and it fails to take into account sufficiently the difficulties in the way of obeying it'.

By the light of this observation, the general interpretation of the Christian message in the context of wealth and poverty can be seen as tending to bear down further on the individual for no good purpose. Such urgings to social conscience are, as Freud suggested, ill adapted to achieve much except an enhancement of social guilt. They attack our individual chances of happiness through selfishness, without telling us how we can achieve happiness in any other way. While adding to our guilt about our own good fortune, they fail to offer a prescription as to how we might relieve the alleged inequality of society. Should I give my money away? What, then, about my children's welfare? And even if I unilaterally decide to do this, what will this achieve other than the microscopic improvement of the situation of perhaps one or two others? Perhaps, it will be countered, I can send a message by my example. But does not the gospel tell me something about not letting the left hand know what the right hand is doing? Should I stop shopping, or shop more quietly, with less obvious enjoyment, perhaps late at night when the stores are quiet? But whom would this benefit, and how?

Our inability to face these questions is Mammon's greatest ally. I am not suggesting that Christianity needs to develop an advanced theory of hedonics, but I do believe it needs to think about the way it contributes to the accumulation of societal guilt without achieving much that might be seen as compensatory benefit. Guilt may cause a degree of what appears to be spontaneous altruism, but more profoundly the action of guilt on the individual is such as to make him unhappy, and unhappy people tend to be less generous, more selfish people.

Capitalism, it now seems clear, is at least slightly better than the alternatives and, in truth, has at its core a spectacularly good idea: that poverty isn't inevitable. There are, in fact, two distinct fundamental ways of seeing the world and its potential to achieve the happiness of all God's children. One is the standard sometimes-Christian/leftist analysis: that the world's resources belong equally to everyone, and any deviation from this principle is a perversion of God's will. The other is that the world's resources are not *ipso facto* the entitlement of anyone because they cannot be marshalled for anyone's benefit unless a sufficiency of humanity can be persuaded to get off its rear end and begin bringing home the bacon. This is what capitalism, at its purest, seeks to do.

It is trite to dismiss the idea of pursuing happiness through consumption, because the idea that this has limits is itself banal. The reality is paradoxical. As Robert E. Lane put it in *The Market Experience*: 'One does not normally think of the market as a moral agent, but indirectly it is one. When it satisfies human wants it increases altruistic behaviour quite outside its own sphere of operations, and its failures contribute to delinquency.'

It is therefore arguable that capitalism, in its essence, is not in conflict with Christianity, but rather an essential prerequisite for the furtherance of the gospel. It is also arguable that the leftist argument about redistribution is out of date in a globalized market, and that Christians who continue to preach those ideas are doing more harm than good. For all its faults, capitalism gets us out of bed in the morning, even if only in pursuit of fleeting illusions. It is fundamentally about the pursuit of happiness, and not necessarily in such a crude manner as its critics maintain. It has this much in common with the Christian message, the core of which is the radical idea that loving my neighbour makes me happier.

It is interesting that stall-holders purveying God or Mammon each accuse the other of peddling illusion. To the 'objective' observer, both have a point: the material is illusion because it ultimately fails to satisfy man's fundamental cravings, and the divine is so because its existence is, even at best, a matter of faith and trust.

But, as even Jesus discovered in the earthly crucible of Gethsemane, the flesh, once assumed, has a pull all but equal to the heavenly dimension. And if this became true for God-made-man, it is infinitely more so for the merely human, for the obvious reason that we lack the certainty of knowing what lies beyond. Man does not live by bread alone. We have heard that message a thousand times, but each time we tend to miss the 'alone'. Our dualistic natures – flesh and spirit – require sustenance from both material and transcendent realities. This surely suggests that it is as natural for the human being to become attached to earthly realities as to long for something beyond. Each of us, to get out of bed in the morning, needs to be impelled in perhaps equal measure by both material considerations, and, even if unconsciously, by something else. The propulsion of the human project requires some combination of both elements, even if one or other is expressed as a negation. The outright atheist and the selfless spiritual ascetic have in common that they seek to defy the natural constraints of the human condition. Each of us, depending on outlook, will see one as virtuous and the other as not, but in truth there is nothing definitively 'good' in either.

Generally – though not invariably – prosperity and secularism seem natural bedfellows. Individuals and societies appear equally prone to abandoning God when their means reach a certain level of plenitude and security. There may be many interconnecting reasons for this. Education, for example, which often flows from growing prosperity, has a tendency to feed in the human mentality an outlook in which the humility that characterizes the believer is diluted or dulled. As we discover more about the world and how it appears to work, we tend to decide that total knowledge is just a matter of time, and that, the way things appear from what we already know, all our previous sense of wonder will one day be debunked. We take out a mortgage on our future all-knowingness and start to live in the here and now in a state predicated on its rather dubious chances of being realized.

But an equally important element of the secularization of the prosperous has to do with guilt, a quality greatly exacerbated in media-saturated societies. Because of the apparent tendency in Christianity to disparage personal wealth and possessions, the maintenance of such becomes increasingly difficult to reconcile with a deep personal faith. With the disparity of means even between members of the same generally prosperous society, one effect of guilt is to force the Haves into a choice: not between keeping their money and giving it away, but between subscribing to a faith that makes them uncomfortable or deciding that they no longer believe in God anyway. And these pressures are infinitely greater in the age of instantaneous globalized images of poverty, famine and catastrophe. The spirit may once have been willing, but the flesh, being weak, has the stronger call on the logic of the prosperous.

The retreat from religion is not merely an expression of postmodern hubris: it is also the expression of a rational self-interest, the desire to escape the contradictions between our lifestyles and what we have been taught to believe. Once faith has been even marginally weakened, the pull of the material is proportionately stronger, and this process is furthered by the continuing message from the open door of the church, from which admonitions about charity pursue the departed doubter as he seeks refuge among his possessions. His response is to become confirmed in his agnosticism. Even from the Christian perspective, it would be better if both God and Mammon could be agreed upon as necessary illusions; from the perspective of society in general, such an attitude would be infinitely preferable to where we are headed now.

The only way for Christianity to combat these tendencies is to begin articulating a way in which Christians might retain a relative level of personal material well-being in a world unequal beyond the individual's ability to influence or alter. The more the old Christian drum is beaten, the more it drives the faithful back to their counting houses.

The culture arising from such influences is hugely deficient in understanding the true psychology of prosperity or in finding practical ways of appropriating its subterranean sentiments. One of its effects is to conceal the degree to which economic disparities in society are the source, even in wealthy individuals, of guilt, sadness, loneliness, and feelings of powerlessness in the face of an unjust world. Concerns about the plight of 'those less fortunate' tend to be placed, on average, midway down (or up) the scale of concerns of the average adult – most others tending to be selfish concerns, such as financial security or personal popularity. Crude left-wing ideas contribute hugely to the sum of such counter-productive sentiment, offering nothing feasible in the way of solution. Much of standard economic theory is unhelpful also, because it focuses excessively on human behaviours attributable to rational self-interest. What this ignores is not so much unselfishness (a moot concept), but the complex ways in which helping others offers a way to feel better. Virtue yields psychic income, and this suggests a whole new way of seeing the issue of redistribution.

A radically different vision may be located behind the pious front of conventional Christianity. In one of his lengthy interviews with the author Peter Seewald, published in 1997 as *Salt of the Earth*, the then Joseph Cardinal Ratzinger used a striking image of the paradox of human prosperity. He referred to the vineyards of Frascati, whose vines bear fruit only if they are pruned once a year. 'If the courage to prune is lacking,' he said, 'only leaves still grow.' He was, naturally, speaking about matters much wider than prosperity – about human desire, the quest for happiness, and the pursuit of material security. Because we are 'built for love', observed the man who would become pope, the refusal to help others is the very ruination of man, for it is 'precisely his submitting himself to a claim and allowing himself to be pruned that enables him to mature and bear fruit'.

# — 8 —
# After Don't

A few years ago, in the course of a casual chat with an Irish Catholic priest of known liberal disposition, it emerged that he believed himself to be at odds with my view of spiritual matters on the basis of having heard me on radio debating with the scientist and theatre director Jonathan Miller. Miller is an atheist and argues forcibly that belief in God is irrational and delusional. The main thrust of my argument against him was that, on the contrary, belief in God is, because it is existentially useful to mankind, a profoundly rational matter. The priest, who would be regarded as a 'liberal' in most matters, found this contention dubious, mainly because he understood me to be talking about social control. 'I don't like this idea that what we are in the business of supplying is a moral framework for society, and that this is the principal benefit of religious faith,' he told me. This is fairly typical of one of the many contortions created in Irish society by the war against Catholicism: liberal Catholics are terrified of being seen any more to seek to impose a theological view on society, and therefore shrink from articulating Catholic principles as a kind of courtesy towards democracy.

Perhaps he misunderstood. My argument was not primarily a social one, but to do with the practical personal benefits of a developed faith. I had in mind the individual rather than society, though there is, of course, another argument to be made about the cumulative societal benefits of individual beliefs. I was arguing against someone who is convinced that faith is mere superstition, and therefore contrary to reason. As a scientist, Jonathan Miller believes in the potential omnipotence of human endeavour. To the extent that he acknowledges a mysterious reality, one gathers that it is merely under the category of 'thus far unexplained'. In our debate, he was remarkably forceful in insisting that 'an intelligent person' must decide against God.

I countered that this is a fatal hubris. The idea that, collectively speaking, we have reached an advanced plane of 'rationality' is bogus. Yes, the world is increasingly technologized; yes, the sum of man's knowledge is increasing. But, each of us, in his or her own life, has access to the merest sliver of this knowledge, and must take most of it on trust, or, if you prefer, faith. Even the sum of our knowledge 'thus far' is so (relatively) limited that there remains far more to be learned than is yet known. To assert, on the basis of a limited, acquired knowledge, that God does not exist, is neither rational nor reasonable. Rather, it is to take out a mortgage on man's potential future knowledge and assume that this, when it arrives, will vindicate human conceits. I had asked Jonathan Miller if, for all his learning, he was capable of creating as much as a fingernail, and he had replied that he was shocked that 'an intelligent person' could believe such nonsense when all his friends were agnostics.

The priest I spoke to, while expressing a liberal reticence, was also articulating something dated and counter-productive in Catholic thinking. At the heart of his difficulty I detected a form of Christian purism, which harks back to something that had long irked me about Irish Catholicism: the insistence that faith is a kind of moral duty, removed from experience and self-interest, which must be practised blindly and without expectation of earthly reward. Perhaps, also, he objected to the idea that, by attributing 'usefulness' to God, I was flirting with the notion of God as a by-product of evolutionary necessity – the idea that, rather than God creating mankind, mankind created God. Primarily, though, I detected in his response a resistance to the notion that, as a priest, his function is primarily sociological, and with this I had some sympathy. As a 'liberal'-minded priest, it is probable that he has spent much energy defending himself against the charge of meddling in social policy, especially in the context of private morality. In my view, the social function of religion is a largely acci-dental by-product of a deep human need. But I also think we should not allow the widespread abuses of the social function of religion to blind us to the profundity of those needs.

Religions generally teach us to think in terms of our duties towards

God, forgetting that what defines our relationship with Him is the knowledge of what He can do for us that we cannot do for ourselves. His most vital role in the lives of human beings is in relieving them of the responsibility to take on the role of God themselves. The important thing is not whether I am sufficiently devout or God is sufficiently happy with my piety, but my awareness of the fact that I myself am not God. I did not make the world and know relatively little about its nature and workings. I could not reconstruct a fingernail on my hand if one happened to fall off. If I cease to believe in God, I am immediately burdened with a responsibility to explain and control, to make the world fall into line with my thinking. God having been pronounced dead or non-existent, a vacancy has arisen on the throne of power, and I am impelled to fill it. Only the constant consciousness that the world is mainly outside my control absolves me from this burden.

This, rather than moral prescriptions or anxiety concerning the afterlife, is by far the most persuasive argument for a functioning godhead: that, if God does not exist, I have an urgent need, in my own interest, to substitute for Him. In the knowledge of God I sleep tightly at night, like a child who knows his parents are asleep in the next room. Without Him, I lie awake fretting about how I might manage or negotiate the world tomorrow.

The Irish Church has not yet woken up to the scale of the anthropological and existential crisis that besets Irish society precisely because of the particular nature of its historical faith experience and its recent rejection of this. A mixture of ignorance, anger, boredom and rebelliousness has caused us to leave Catholicism behind in the manner of someone who throws away his umbrella because it has stopped raining. Convinced that only the diktats of joyless greybeards stood between us and the earthly attainment of paradise, we rejoice in the discomfiture of Catholicism and take our pleasure where we will. In the early flushes of freedom, we are deaf to any possibility that we have lost something of use in what we have left behind.

The very refuge we have chosen from traditional austerity is now beset by dilemmas and contradictions for which, of all the philosophies we have encountered and tried out, only faith offers the possibility of relief. The primary difficulty with the alleged rationality of our age is not that it denies God the belief and loyalty of humanity, but that it denies humanity the knowledge and protection of God. And the only conceivable way we might get around this is to somehow convince this 'rational' and self-interested age that there is a benefit to be gained from believing. If the Catholic Church wishes to overcome the spirit of this age, it must set aside both its purism and its apolitical pieties and start to talk up the practical benefits of belief.

A major difficulty, as I have outlined, has to do with what I would call the 'mental age' of Irish society. The young tend to be curious and wonderstruck, and these qualities are well attuned to seeking out hope. The old may be weary but have accumulated wisdoms based on their mistakes. The difficulty is that Ireland is defined at present by the thinking of middle age. Too old for curiosity, too young to be alerted to the folly of its own errors, it blunders about in the fog of its own omniscience and certainty.

The Church, in this analogy, represents the wisdom of maturity. In metaphysical terms, many of the Church's teachings relate to a paradox of human living that reveals itself only with age: the promise of the appetite that thunders through the veins of the young is deceptive as to the earthly outcome. The irrefutable earthly wisdom of this message resides in its capacity to protect, in its accumulated understanding of the cost of freedom for the individual, and in its tendering of the serenity offered by a faith-based propriety as the only possibility of quelling or supplanting the human appetite for sensation. The philosophy of Free Love tells us that the negative consequences of the pursuit of gratification are the result of repression or bad luck; Catholic theology tells us they are the unavoidable backlash of a thirst that is unquenchable. But Irish Catholicism simply tells us that sex outside marriage is 'immoral'. We throw our eyes up to heaven and continue our search for a better explanation or a more efficient form of freedom. The essential problem with Irish Catholicism is not that it is out of date but that it is neither understood by those who might gain from it, nor properly explained by those seeking to promote it. Many aspects of the Catholic message have been over-simplified for mass consumption into a series of prescriptions and proscriptions, in which the core metaphysical wisdoms are dulled or obscured. The origins of this condition are to be found in Ireland's history of radical interference from outside. Before Irish Catholicism could adjust, the arrival of mass education, hotly followed by the sudden enrichment of Irish society, pulled the rug from under this simple edifice of rules and values. Catholic 'Don'ts', often unadorned by rationalization or explanation, were a poor match for the sixties' message of individualism and Free Love. For educated young people, it was no longer enough to be assured that something was sinful: there was a need also to outline the earthly logic for abstinence, and this was rarely, or badly, done.

So also with money. A poor agnostic, convinced the misery of his earthly life is related to his finances, has the hope of getting rich. A rich agnostic benefits from no such illusion. Each new day he needs to invent further targets of acquisition to keep at bay the encroaching sense of meaninglessness which grows with the zeros on his bottom line. An over-simplification of the Christian message has served to obscure that one of the key functions of faith is its animation of the believer with reasons to go on living.

We are for the moment unable to see the precise dangers of a general loss of faith, because the logic of individualism assures us that each individual has the opportunity to control his own spiritual destiny, and that the option of a transcendent outlook can be adopted on a pick-and-mix basis – 'I used to be a Catholic, but now I'm a Buddhist.' While this may work for individuals, it hardly ever works for societies, because a culture formed in the crucible of a particular faith cannot simply jettison that faith and adopt another.

Nor can a society successfully remain agnostic in the way an individual may seem to. The unbelieving individual, in a broadly believing society, can function well by availing himself of the slipstream and buffering provided by the faith of others (in a sense, as suggested earlier, the unbeliever is a parasite on the belief of his neighbours); an overwhelmingly unbelieving society, once it exhausts the imaginative possibilities of money and other freedoms, is doomed to a form of collective depression.

Perhaps these, rather than the threat of damnation or the loss of what we conventionally think of as moral values, are the factors that will, one day, cause us to ask what became of that bath, and that baby we threw out with that bathwater.

When people ask me how they might find their way back to faith, I tell them to fake it till they make it, because that worked for me: first

171

I looked for the utilitarian meaning of the supernatural — of ritual, prayer and faith – and in doing so found a way back to the mechanisms by which mankind had traditionally sought to override its own lack of omnipotence, which is to say by installing a godhead to 'explain' and dominate the mysterious parts of the world. Pre-rational man, deciding that he needed to know a higher being than himself in order to live coherently on the earth with a minimum of terror and confusion, may well have imagined a God, which became gods, but then, needing to eliminate the memory of his invention so as to believe completely in his concept, forgot that he had invented it, inveigling himself into a superstition that lifted the weight of self-deception from his heart. On the other hand, if his intuition was correct, wasn't it possible that God had created his mind so as to perform precisely this loop of reasoning? In abolishing God, we imagined we would become more free, but this freedom has been swamped by the unanticipated imposition on disbelieving man of a legion of unaccounted responsibilities and anxieties that previously were the business of the Almighty. With the arrival of what we nowadays rather presumptuously call the modern era (broadly, the post-1960s period), posterity, imagining itself to be infinitely clever, dismissed this superstition, discovered that God did not, in fact, exist, and promptly abolished Him. In doing so, man was set promptly back to the point where he began, his terror and confusion returned, and he knew not why.

The most important discovery I made on the journey was that I didn't have to be so clever, intuiting that, far from it being clever to disbelieve in God, scepticism and agnosticism may be pointless and dangerous vanities. Perhaps the smartest of all people are those who can overcome their intelligence to an extent that allows them to believe.

What was a few years ago an issue for me is now a daily issue for Ireland. A decade ago, in *An Intelligent Person's Guide to Modern Ireland* (Duckworth, 1977), I outlined the sociological profile of a condition then only beginning to attract notice. I don't propose to repeat or to update the statistical picture I outlined then – suffice it to say in tandem with the increasing affluence of recent years, the previous 'myth' of the drunken Irish has been acquiring an alarming degree of substance and truth. Formerly, the notion of the inebriated Irishman may have had a great deal to do with the image of the lonesome Irish emigrant, crying into his beer in Kilburn or Boston or Toronto. But whereas the statistics in the past did not bear out this image with regard to the home territory, increasingly they do. Today, Ireland, North and South, is close to the top of the European league in alcohol consumption. In that book of a decade ago I referred to a Department of Health document on alcohol policy which blithely declared that 'there is evidence that the depiction of the Irish as a particularly alcohol-prone race is a myth'. With politicians and social commentators now openly talking about 'the national alcohol problem', it is clear that we have travelled a long way in a relatively short time in the perception of addiction in our midst.

But there is as yet a reluctance to make the broadest appropriate connections, or to extend the discussion to enable a proper understanding of the nature of what lies behind all such headlines: the growing propensity of Irish people to this and other forms of addiction. A newer phenomenon, noticeable in recent times, is the theme of obesity – not as yet being linked to the alcohol problem. While there are evolving discussions about problematic aspects of our increased consumption of, for example, alcohol, drugs and sugar, there is as yet no movement towards the integration of these matters under their common heading.

The cultural attitude towards alcohol in Ireland tends to oscillate between two diametrically removed points. On the one hand, we tend to be tolerant beyond prudence of those who over-indulge. In this part of our collective brain, we imagine that a tendency towards drunkenness is, if a flaw at all, a flaw to be indulged. But occasionally, when things get out of hand, we lurch off into total intolerance, demanding that those who appear to take our first response too literally be brought to account for their conduct.

If alcoholism is indeed a disease – and six decades of experience tells us that we should be loathe to dismiss this ideas outright – then intolerance and punitive methods aimed at those suffering from alcoholism are, firstly, doomed to failure; secondly, liable to wrongly exculpate society in an unhelpful way; and, thirdly, short-circuit the learning process at both individual and collective levels. To describe alcoholism as a disease is far from suggesting that we are powerless to overcome it. And if alcoholism is a disease besetting the individual – and this is a useful way of seeing things with a view to formulating a treatment – then it is reasonable to conclude that disproportionate consumption of alcohol in the collective dimension amounts to a national pathology. Already, in the belated responses to this well-established crisis, we observe our own desire to obfuscate and deny this possibility. The standard analysis is that alcohol consumption, even to considerable excess, is a symptom primarily of enjoyment, with a few debauched individuals contriving to spoil the party for everyone else. This viewpoint would seek, up to a very stretched point, to interpret the alarmingly increased consumption levels of recent years as evidence of a somewhat unabashed celebration of national prosperity. But the statistics suggest that the relationship between the consumption of alcohol and increased wealth is not so straightforward. Over the past decade or so, more affluent households and individuals have consumed more alcohol than before, but the most significant increases in spending on alcohol have tended to be in the lower socio-economic groupings, which manifest a more increased relative expenditure on drink than the more comfortable classes. The sole exception to this pattern is among small farmers and agricultural workers, whose drinking patterns have not altered significantly.

A crude analysis of this might be that the increased consumption of alcohol in Irish society, and the epidemic of alcoholism which accompanies it, are the symptoms, not so much of increased prosperity, as of increased alienation from the society which prosperity has delivered. We need a new word for this, since 'alienation' has been rendered meaningless by the dead-hand of Marx, and another alternative, 'anomie', is too opaque and pretentious to be of any use in the project of popular enlightenment. Identified by the French sociologist Emile Durkheim, 'anomie' is a condition afflicting societies where the normative regulation of relationships by rules and values has collapsed, resulting in individual feelings of despair, isolation and meaninglessness which surface in the form of various social disorders such as those that now manifestly beset Irish society. There can be little doubt that the national alcohol problem amounts to such a symptom. The physical and mental symptoms of the disease of alcoholism are, in the individual, the manifestation of the spiritual paraplegia besetting the collective to which he or she belongs. Durkheim called it 'the malady of infinite aspiration', the condition of wanting more and more of what fails to answer your questions. Such ideas are regularly canvassed in Irish public debate, but rarely taken seriously, partly because they seem too fanciful and partly because any deeper exploration of them would take us into national pain.

Alcohol abuse occurs in conditions exhibiting fairly clear-cut common characteristics and symptoms. For its abusers, alcohol becomes not a social lubricant or an enhancer of enjoyment but an analgesic and substitute for meaning. If this is true for the individual, there is every reason to hold that it may also be true of society. Alcoholism, then, may be a disease with a social life as well as an individual dimension. In other words, there are such things as alcoholic cultures, Ireland being one such. I believe that, like Native American and other aboriginal peoples, and for much the same reasons, we have been rendered disproportionately susceptible to the disease of alcoholism, and that both genetic elements and cultural factors feed this condition.

One rationalization of the phenomenon of recent Irish drinking relates to the undeniable fact that the preponderance of the problem resides in the younger age groups. This has caused some observers to point to a more hopeful trend. The argument goes something like this: since the vast bulk of the increase in consumption has occurred in the 18–34 age groups, Irish demographic patterns do not necessarily lend themselves to doomsday comparisons with other countries. Because the proportion of the Irish population in the 18–34 range is much higher than in other countries in Europe, there is quite a prosaic explanation for why alcohol consumption has risen dramatically in Ireland while declining elsewhere. The population bulge resulting from the delayed baby boom has recently moved into the natural heavy-drinking age range and will shortly begin to move on into the more moderate drinking patterns of middle age.

In statistical terms the picture is precisely so. But the analysis rests on the assumption that excessive drinking, because it has manifested itself primarily in the younger age groups, is a kind of lifestyle option, a phase the young are going through. It emphasizes the circumstantial patterns, while overlooking both the cultural nature of Irish society and the reasons why people drink to excess. Irish society is culturally middle-aged, but one of its symptoms is a block that seems to prevent people, young or not-so-young, from growing up. For the society to be able to begin treating its maladies, there would need to be a great deal more awareness of the precise nature of these maladies than there currently is. One of the problems arising from the prolonged excessive consumption of alcohol is the emotional retardation that this inflicts. A person who is avoiding life's difficulties by numbing the everyday pain and fear of living under a poultice of alcohol is not growing in a manner that might remotely be described as normal. In our failure, then, to properly examine this issue, we are bequeathing to our children a form of emotional and social retardation, both by virtue of our failure to understand the nature of alcohol and by our refusal to manage its effects on society. Our children are being denied the opportunities to grow as full human beings, uninhibited and unimpeded by a drug which, being a depressant, stifles their natural impulses, creativity and learning processes.

What worries me is how faithfully the patterns to be observed in Irish society seem to follow my own early adult steps. When I drank myself into meaninglessness, I too was between 18 and 35. My story, at the surface level, might be taken as reassurance that the binge drinkers of today will also grow out of it. Except that I didn't grow out of it. You don't 'grow' out of alcohol abuse, at least not in the sense of just waiting for some physical change to take you beyond the obsession or the danger zone. Growth has a lot to do with it, but it is a different kind of growth and it doesn't just happen.

What evidence we have concerning the collapse of belief in God in Irish society displays enormous circumstantial conformity with the increasing abuse of alcohol and drugs.

A survey of third-level educated young adults between the ages of 20 and 35, conducted by Desmond O'Donnell, OMI, and published in the January 2002 edition of *Doctrine and Life*, presented a fascinating sketch of the spiritual outlook of the young. In general terms, about two in five respondents appeared to have no belief in a spiritual dimension. Of these a majority were male, with younger males being significantly more likely to lack such belief. For example, 5 per cent of males, but only 3 per cent of females, declared an outright denial of life after death, and those between 20 and 25 were four times more prone to such a view than those aged between 30 and 35. Asked to choose between 12 possible descriptions of their experience of God, the respondents displayed a similar pattern, with the 20–30 age group being less likely to accept descriptions like 'peace', 'trust', and 'being loved'. Negative experiences of God were more common among males, with 8 per cent of males, as against 3 per cent of females, agreeing to the term 'nothing' as a description of their relationship with God.

In general, the worst abuses of alcohol occur among males in their early twenties, the cohort in which belief in a spiritual dimension is most lacking. This is not a coincidence. And since such unbelief is a relatively new and growing phenomenon, and since alcohol abusers do not suddenly convert to moderate consumption on reaching a certain age, and since experience tells us that God is not miraculously restored to the lives of adults without some profound transformation occurring, it is likely that, far from dissipating when the present demographic bulge passes into middle age, our national alcohol problem will continue to grow and grow.

Alcoholism is not about alcohol. Addiction is not about addiction. Our collective concepts in this connection are way out of date: the unemployed drug addict, the wino in the gutter with his bottle of plonk. Growing comprehension that food, for example, also has highly addictive properties must surely shift our perceptions of the issue towards some understanding of an underlying condition, but this is a relatively new shift and comes on top of the old misunderstandings.

We have tended, thus far, to see the relevant substance-of-choice as itself representing the problem. But this inverts the puzzle of addiction, which is best understood in terms of the void it has developed to fill. Alcohol and drugs are very effective at temporarily restoring missing bits of the human psychic mechanism. Ask any heroin addict and you'll be told that heroin does exactly what it says on the bag. But because these substances are also poisons, their positive effect is short-lived and far outweighed by the negatives. Experience tells us that addicts are not just hapless individuals who happen to develop a damaging fondness for a harmful substance – but, more importantly, damaged souls who achieve wholeness only through their addiction.

We also urgently need to pursue a more functional comprehension of the societal conditions pushing young people towards such dependencies. The problem is not simply advertising or the prevalence of money, or the easy availability of this or that drink or substance. We need to consider, perhaps, in what ways our culture is failing to feed the spiritual life of the young. We fight increasingly sophisticated and pernicious foes for the lives of our children, and we need to start thinking a lot more cleverly. The most urgent need, therefore, is to bring together the various forms of expertise – from the medical, socio-cultural and spiritual disciplines – with a view to answering a question broadly along the lines of: 'Why have we come to fear living so much that we choose to kill ourselves slowly in the guise of enjoying ourselves?'

The assassination of God has had some weird and unexpected consequences, one of which is the effect of manmade 'gods' on the consciousness of the individual. One of the problems associated with modern living has undoubtedly to do with the pejorative comparison to be made between the 'ordinary' individual and the 'celebrity' who is in our faces all day, every day. My parents' generation faced nothing like this: they 'knew' perhaps a few dozen people and were able to deal with any sense of comparative inadequacy by counterbalancing one quality against another. Even when I was at school, the problem was just beginning to manifest itself in the burgeoning obsession of the young with soccer players and pop stars. The altered nature of public culture, arising from television, movies and celebrity magazines causes young people to grow up in a context of 'competition' with all kinds of high-profile celebrities and others, whose public profiles stem from excellence or achievement in some field or other. Without proper skills of evaluation and comparison, and without a broad sense of what life is about, young people are driven in this celebrity culture to building fantasies which, by virtue of being in most cases unattainable, render that person at some future point susceptible to considerable life disappointment which may be ameliorated through drugs or alcohol. Dreams and illusions are healthy aspects of living. But for someone who, by his own lights, is unable to live up to his dreams, the lure of drugs and alcohol is very tempting. And because so much of our sense of personal motivation depends on ambitions and dreams, the insertion of a powerful chemical into the equation can often short-circuit such motivation and create an artificial dependency which initially is less an addiction to the substance than to its effects. For many young people nowadays life can be like a lottery, with at least a viable chance of becoming 'somebody'. Such illusion keeps many of us going to a far greater extent than we imagine. We build our dreams on the clouds above our heads, set our caps in that direction and strike onwards in hope. The failure of this mechanism is the key to what we know as alcoholism.

The world knows little of this disease, imagining it crudely as some inexplicable dependence on a substance others can take or leave. But it is more than that: drugs are a death-delaying short-circuit for despair, the refuge of those who have lived or dreamt things that surpass their expectations. Alcoholism happens to people when they reach a point where the future seems more pointless than the past.

We need to understand more about what motivates young people, especially I believe, young men, who, for example, don't have any culture of responsible parenthood to hook into. If they can't achieve their dreams on the sports field or at work, they've basically had it, and the bottle offers hope of peace or redemption. We need to look at an education system geared to producing units for the workplace rather than people who can live good lives. We need to re-evaluate the concepts of happiness with which we bombard ourselves and our young, and perhaps even substitute them with the concept of peace, a different philosophical basis. And we need to remember that alcohol and drugs are very effective short-term means of restoring the missing bits of the human psychic mechanism.

Perhaps the most unhelpful, if not damaging, word in Irish political discourse in my lifetime has been the word 'moral'. Time and again, we have engaged in discussions about whether or not we should go the 'modern' way or the 'moral' way, when really we should have been talking about what was useful. It has often struck me, for example, that debates about the 'liberal agenda' have been won, not on objective merits, but largely on the back of a neurotic reaction against Catholicism. Because the counter arguments originated in Catholic traditionalism, it was easy to present the liberal agenda as representing some more modern, progressive and beneficially liberating option. At issue, we came to believe, was whether or not we wanted a bunch of misanthropic, dandruffed old men to continue dictating how we should live our lives. During the divorce referendums, for example, the discussion became embroiled in the 'moral' dimensions of marital break-up, when really the focus needed to be on the functionality of a society in which divorce was available. The debate was therefore dominated by false opposites: church teaching versus personal rights and 'compassion'. A more useful discussion would have been defined by a different set of opposites: personal rights versus a concept of collective rights centred on the idea that, though ostensibly individuated, human beings achieve autonomy in harmony with their society or not at all.

Most of us no longer hear this language of 'morality' as we did a generation ago. Then, we were inside the tent of whatever logic pertained; now, most of us are outside. In Ireland the relationship of the general public to the Catholic Church and its personnel is ambivalent at best, and increasingly hostile in the main. Today, when an Irish Catholic hears a priest complain about the dangers of a general loss of morality or faith, he or she hears only a self-interested lamentation or an admonition of the ebbing tide. When the speaker makes a connection between godlessness and public decadence, moral blackmail is suspected: reject the Church and you will rue the day! Those still inside the tent nod sanctimoniously and cast their eyes upwards; the rest shrug complacently, sensing the dismay of a cleric at the decline of his business. The general neurosis and sense of resentment about the Church leads people either to reject the message or apprehend its delivery in a way that discounts the cost of disbelief to the disbelieving. We hear in any attempt to invoke religious or spiritual values, or warn of the consequences of their decline, only the vested interest of a vanquished institution seeking to bring us back to our knees.

That we are brought to our knees in manifold other ways (not least by drink at two in the morning) is treated as the inevitable collateral damage of 'progress' or as a dissociated phenomenon of ambiguous meaning. Our dominant sense is not that we have lost control of ourselves, which might strike us as bad, but that 'They' have lost control of us, which seems to us to be good. There exists no neutral voice to assert that the problem is perhaps that we have sought to gain excessive control of ourselves, that, in banishing God from His throne, we have burdened ourselves with more than we can handle. What we are becoming, therefore, is neither progressive nor accidental, but an inevitable consequence of the loss of God, which has deprived us of a view of any absolute horizon of human capability. In this, we need urgently to perceive that the primary damage is to ourselves, with the hurt to the Church, in which so many of us take a perverse pleasure, being very much a collateral phenomenon. And without such a voice, we are unable to perceive that this is primarily an issue of societal mechanics. Our hostility to Catholicism leads us to reject the thought that we have lost something of practical use to ourselves, or to acknowledge that the pietistic language of 'traditional' Irish Catholicism, which now offends us by its simplicity and its prescriptiveness, is just a particular way of invoking a deity upon the knowledge of Whom the human species depends in manifold ways.

The Irish Catholic commentator David Quinn has drawn a rather fascinating analogy between Ireland's relationship with England and Irish society's relationship with the Catholic Church. His analysis, broadly, is that, since the trauma of our relationship with the colonial power which dominated us for centuries has mellowed into a cordial equality, there is no reason – despite falling church attendance and other downbeat indicators – to be pessimistic about the prospects of healing between Irish society and the Church.

The comparison is apt, though not exactly a parallel. Although much crude popular sociology would have it so, the dominance of the Catholic Church in Ireland was never a colonial presence: the equation of Whitehall with the Vatican does not quite stack up. While in some respects it is impossible to deny the validity of the 'Rome rule' catcall, so much favoured by Northern Unionists, it is only one perspective on the story. From another direction it has to be acknowledged that the Church since the Famine has been a kind of anti-colonial power, offering a focus for the marshalling of indigenous energies, and providing an emblem of authentic difference for the native population.

This had a massively negative side. The Catholic Church, in the absence of political leadership or any form of self-determination after the Great Famine, took on the role of surrogate moral government – greatly to the detriment of both society and the faith. At the time there may well have been no alternative, but the consequences are still being lived and dealt with, as the legacy of the escalation of church power continues to ricochet around the society. The blurring of the pastoral and social roles of the Church has been the source of much of the resentment it now attracts. The truth, then, is paradoxical: the Church was both protector and, in a different sense, oppressor.

There are indeed many striking similarities to the colonial equation. Colonialism operates in a profound manner to recondition the mind of the colonized against himself. As Frantz Fanon wrote in *The Wretched of the Earth*, the first thing the colonizer does is convince the native that, before the advent of colonialism 'there was nothing but savagery'. This creates an imperative to obtain the approval of the colonizer, to follow his prescriptions and to emulate him in every possible way. Some will always remain free, or relatively free, from this process, but if it is successful in infecting a critical mass of the population, it can both redefine the entire society and still manage to conceal itself from those affected by it. Underneath the denial is a host of complexes, resentments, neuroses and rages, which, because they have no means of being directed at what has actually provoked them, tend to lash out in all directions.

It's only really in the past decade or so that Irish society has begun to awaken to the fact that it was actually colonized in the first place, and this process of awakening has, remarkably, been accompanied by a melting away of the underlying resentments. Our relationship with England is today better than it has ever been. This is partly because of the cessation of activity by the Provisional IRA, but also because, in the growing self-confidence arising from prosperity, we no longer feel like the hick relation in the presence of our sophisticated former masters. Now we are not only beginning to acknowledge the wealth and complexity of cultural value that has accrued in Ireland as a result of English interference, but also to develop a way of acknowledging this while remaining clear about the immorality of that interference. It is a complicated thing. Our new embrace of our neighbour is not the outcome of a superficial, maudlin desire for reconciliation at all costs, but of a mature and complex understanding of what happened, and how this fits into the complex fabric of real life. We are not so much forgiving and forgetting as re-embracing while remembering more clearly.

I believe David Quinn is right that something similar will happen between Irish society and the Church: that there will come a time when the role of Catholicism in Irish society will no longer trigger the cultural neurosis it now does, and when the Catholic Church will again be able to dispense its message without apology and have it accepted as yet another worthwhile contribution to the marketplace of ideas in the public square.

Extending his analogy, David asked how long this might be likely to take, and, more precisely, what might be the corresponding point in this connection to the Declaration of Independence in 1921. Various moments suggest themselves: the abortion referendum, the divorce amendment, the infamous 'X Case' of the 1990s which provoked yet another national controversy about abortion, moments when the neurotic liberal resistance to alleged Church interference and oppressiveness claimed signal victories. But I would identify a different moment: the cultural banishment of Eamonn Casey, the Bishop of Galway, who in 1992 was revealed to have fathered a child with an American woman and to have misappropriated diocesan funds to pay for the boy's education. This represented not merely a 'victory' for liberals, but also a dramatization of that victory in a way that was perhaps both necessary and potentially redemptive. The outing of a 'hypocritical' bishop was at the time a cataclysmic episode for both the opponents of the Church and those who sought to defend what was good in Catholicism. But perhaps equally cataclysmic has been the recent return of Bishop Casey, in a spirit of contrition, to an embrace of empathy and reconciliation. What Bishop Casey, by living his human weaknesses in the public domain and facing their consequences, had shown was what Pope Benedict XVI called 'the courage to be imperfect', and in doing so he created a visible dramatization of something happening at a deeper level.

Perhaps the most misleading and distracting myth about the relationship between Irish society and Catholicism is the idea that the falling away from the Church, particularly by younger people, has been to do with what are termed 'the scandals' – clerical sexual abuse, institutional abuses and the attempts at suppression and cover-up which tended to follow from such episodes. My own experience of faith and its loss makes obvious to me that this analysis puts the cart before the horse. Pious and devout as a child and teenager, at 19 I hit a wall, not primarily of disbelief but of disillusion. I recognize it retrospectively as following much the same path as the disillusion Irish society began to go through in the 1990s, with the beginning of the 'Church scandals'. My resentment of a single arbitrary exercise of clerical authority, combined with a degree of underground intelligence about that particular cleric's private behaviour, led me to the 'obvious' conclusion: they were all at it, all the same, and God might be no better.

The undoubted waning of the influence of Catholicism in Ireland in the past two to three decades has to do with much deeper matters, of which the abuses and cover-ups were often merely further symptoms. Many people, it is true, advance their disquiet at these events as the rationale for their personal sense of disillusionment, but, in many instances, I believe, this is either disingenuousness, intellectual laziness or outright self-delusion. It's much easier to put one's loss of belief or conviction down to something manifest and encapsulated within a neat common shorthand than to get into understanding and explaining the deeper reality.

The common link between the accepted explanation and the deeper truth probably resides in the nature of the Irish Church, which for at least a century and a half had placed authority and obedience before other considerations. The conditions deriving from this climate of authoritarianism acted not merely to create the conditions in which abuses were inevitable, but also sowed the seeds of unbelief in the hearts of the people. Put simply, the relationship between Church and people became excessively analogous to a parent–child relationship. Simple verities, expressed as iron prescriptions and proscriptions, became the core of Irish Catholicism's intellectual content.

When I was teenager, we had a priest who came into the school to teach us Christian Doctrine (not the one who subsequently triggered my own moment of schism). Anxious to engage in arguments about the manifest clash between church teachings and the nature of the world we were beginning to inhabit, we would throw questions at him. Why this? Why not that? Who says? And so forth. His answer was always the same: 'Because it's the law of God.' This communicated to us that the Church had no answers to questions about the dissonances between real life and religious belief.

For my own part then (and I feel that this is true for a great many others), unbelief became synonymous with finding my own answers. In front of me was a world crying out to be understood, taken on, accommodated to, embraced; behind me was a Church which said that the way to deal with the issues and difficulties of the world was to avoid them, to mutter a few pious ejaculations in moments of stress or temptation and, where tensions arose between what I had been taught and what I encountered, to assume that the answers were more likely to be found in the simple verities than in any more complex engagement of my own intellectual faculties. It was not long before I came to regard this set of prescriptions as completely useless as a toolkit for modern living. Catholicism became not merely a redundant programme but in many ways an embarrassment. To profess belief was to admit to a lack of independent-mindedness or intellectual ambition, to advertise what would only be read externally as simplicity of outlook. To be a practising Catholic was to appear to be, in some ways, weak and backward. To be a non-believer, however, was to advertise what seemed to be various forms of strength: independence of mind, courage, intelligence, progressiveness, self-belief, confidence in one's place in the world. It was to be unafraid, to be reliant on one's own resources and to attract around oneself both others of like mind and those of less-developed assuredness.

When I hear talk about the 'Enlightenment split' and the modern shift from faith to rationality, this memory of my own searching is the only tangible meaning it has for me. I, for my part, abandoned belief, not because of things individuals clerics might have done, but because I found the modern world seductive and felt the Church did not seem to know very much about it. And, having found my way within the modern world – up to a point – I felt vindicated in my choices throughout my youth and well into adulthood.

It has taken me a very long time to even begin to unpick these determinations. I wandered back in some confusion, having discovered the limits of my own resources, to find that, like Mark Twain's father, the Church appeared to have learned much in my absence. To read today the writings of John Paul II or Benedict XVI is to tumble across the answers we were looking for in those Christian doctrine classes all those years ago, and also to discover sharply articulated explanations for our failure to find what we were looking for in exile. 'We see the self-confidence of modernity increasingly crumble,' said Joseph Cardinal Ratzinger to Peter Seewald in his book-length interview *Salt of the Earth*. 'For it is becoming clearer and clearer that progress also involves progress in the powers of destruction, that ethically man is not equal to his own reason.'

It is, of course, the law of God, but if we could have been told such things in something like that way when we were caught up in the questions of youth, perhaps we might never have felt the need to wander off.

Then, in the early-to-mid-1990s, I noticed that more and more people were following the path I had taken. It has seemed to me since then that the reasons people offer for their decision to walk away from the Church are not entirely truthful. People say they are disillusioned with the dissonance between message and behaviour, or claim they resent the unwarranted intrusion on private morality which religion has come to signify in their lives. Really, I believe these are post hoc rationalizations for something that happened a long time before. I have no doubt they resented the limitations that religion places on their behaviour, but the real problem, as in my own life, was that such restrictions no longer appeared to have any counter-balancing compensations. When you take away the force of the authority, the 'Don'ts', the guilt and the fear of punishment, there is nothing, or not enough, remaining to amount to a reason to stay with something that seems to be primarily about denying elements of your humanity. The question for Irish Catholicism, then, is: what comes after 'Don't'?

I don't claim my experience as in any sense prophetic. Rather, what I believe is that, because of the nature of mass-media society, there is a time-lag between what happens in the recesses of the human soul and the expression of this happening in the public consciousness. I suspect that my own experience of rejecting Catholicism coincided with a more general phenomenon of a similar kind, but that this did not find pubic expression until triggered by a series of clerical scandals nearly two decades later. Strangely, too, as society in its public manifestation was beginning to follow this course, I was beginning to turn back in search of some lost, half-remembered thread from the past. This leads me to wonder if something similar is not happening in the hearts of many others as well.

In his book *The Hundredth Monkey*, Ken Keyes Jr. writes about a phenomenon which, he believes, may be our only hope as a species. In 1952, on the Japanese island of Koshima, scientists were feeding monkeys of the breed *macaca fuscata* with seed potatoes dropped on the sand. The monkeys liked the sweet potatoes, but not the sand in which they were coated. There was a problem: how to make the potatoes palatable. An 18-month-old monkey called Imo came up with the answer: she washed the potatoes in a stream, and taught her mother to do the same. Likewise her playmates, who also passed the trick on to their mothers. Scientists watched as this discovery was relayed through the colony of monkeys. In the course of the next six years, all the young monkeys learned to wash the potatoes in this way. Only those adults who imitated their young learned to wash the potatoes; the remainder continued eating them with their coating of sand. Then, wrote Keyes, something startling occurred. 'In the autumn of 1958, a certain number of Koshima monkeys were washing sweet potatoes – the exact number is not known. Let us suppose that when the sun rose one morning there were 99 monkeys on Koshima island who had learned to wash their sweet potatoes. Let's further suppose that later that morning, the hundredth monkey learned to wash potatoes. Then it happened.' By that evening almost every member of the colony was washing the potatoes prior to eating. The point of the story? 'The added energy of this hundredth monkey somehow created an ideological breakthrough.' In other words, with the winning over of the hundredth monkey, some kind of critical mass point had been reached.

There was more. 'The most surprising thing observed by these scientists', wrote Keyes, 'was that the habit of washing sweet potatoes then spontaneously jumped over the sea – colonies of monkeys on other islands and the mainland troop of monkeys at Takasakiyama began washing their sweet potatoes.'

The meaning of this? 'When a certain number achieves an aware-ness, this new awareness may be communicated from mind to mind. Although the exact number may vary, the Hundredth Monkey Phenomenon means that when only a limited number of people know of a new way, it may remain the conscious property of these people. But there is a point at which if only one more person tunes into a new awareness, a field is strengthened so that this awareness reaches almost everyone.'

There are particular reasons for predicting that this syndrome may yet manifest itself in the matter of the Irish people's relationship with faith and Church. One reason I say this is because I have noted so often the extent of the divergence between what Irish people tend to say to each other in private conversation, the kinds of things they say to me, for example, when the subject of religion comes up, and what the collective voice offered by the Irish media would have them believe. The strange thing about the mass media is that, far from pro-moting diversity, they seem to cause the mainstream view to become narrower and more monolithic, like a dam forcing water into one single torrent. And such is the force of this view that, in general, people tend not to challenge it. The result is that the personal views, perspectives and beliefs of the individual are repressed out of hearing, driven, as it were, back into the heart.

This process is accelerated by the separating effect of modern media. The construction of our public thinking apparatus, the way we dispense and acknowledge the right to be known as 'expert', our com-partmentalization of public discussions in a way that replicates the character of a newspaper, are all suggestive of a secret desire to hide meanings from ourselves. Each discipline of public thought has acquired an excluding language, further hindering a conversation in which the threads of meaning might be drawn together. Here, we have the priests, sermonizing about sanctity and grace; there, the soci-ologists, discoursing about technocratic solutions. Each maintains a stern hostility towards anyone who would step into his turf without appropriate apparel and qualifications. This hostility goes beyond protectionism, amounting almost to an expression of the societal desire to deny the interconnectedness of things. Thus, the vested interest of the professional in maintaining the exclusivity of his practice becomes the mechanism by which society prevents a decline into a chaotic, democratic argument, which might, in approaching sense, undo the commodification of knowledge on which control of society's culture and conventional wisdom depends.

In the early weeks and months of the papacy of Benedict XVI it became striking that he seemed continually to use a word we had previously associated with Catholic clerics more as a description than as an utterance. The word was 'boredom'. All my life, it had seemed that boredom was the prescribed demeanour for the conscientious Christian: if you weren't bored, you weren't doing it right. But Benedict XVI suggested otherwise: he seemed to believe that boredom is symptomatic of something unhelpful. As Cardinal Ratzinger, he could almost be said to have sprinkled the word through his writings. He uses it to describe the demeanour of modern youth, the effect of changes in Catholic liturgy, the poisoning and trivialization of human love by egotism and lust and the consequences of a relativist tendency in thinking which reduces every concept to a cycle of experimental reflection and subjective apprehension. We are, he says, bored by our lives, bored by our attempts to relieve our boredom, bored by religion, bored by our own thoughts.

Rocco Buttiglione, a theologian, philosopher, sometime politician, and confidant of both John Paul II and Benedict XVI, when asked to explain why so many young people seemed to love Pope John Paul II, said that nowadays we find ourselves stuck in 'a Kingdom of Boredom' and that John Paul had shown them a way out. Refining this idea somewhat, Charles Moore, a late convert to Catholicism, wrote in the *Daily Telegraph* that, in the absence of a single identifiable monarch, 'Republic of Boredom' might be a better phrase. It seemed to be the perfect phrase to describe the country in which I grew up.

Boredom, wrote Moore, means the mood that comes from pointlessness: 'Its symptoms are everywhere – at airports, in screens in bars which no one is watching, in channel-hopping, in shopping malls, in the halitosis that breathes from the doors of fast-food outlets, in the obsession with body weight. It's in astrology, in talking about football because you think you're supposed to, in *Big Brother*, in waiting for the results of the National Lottery, in recreational drugs and binge-drinking, in the devout political/commercial belief that no one has an attention span of more than twenty seconds, and, to be honest, in a great deal of feeble religious liturgy.

'Young people are more the victims of this boredom than any other group, because advertisers and politicians regard them as persuadable.' The young themselves, 'in some respects more conformist than older people, punish those of their number who do not respond to these calls – the requirement to be cool being the most coercive of all 21st-century social pressures'.

It was a brilliant description of the phenomenon's symptoms, but less than enlightening about the cause. For this we must look to the words of Joseph Ratzinger. Addressing himself to the phenomenon of student-left radicalism that swept Europe in the late 1960s, and which had its echo in what I have called the Peter Pan revolution that transformed Ireland in the 1970s and 1980s, he observed that Western youth's clamouring for freedom was a measure, not of their imprisonment, still less of their passion for the downtrodden other, but of their cosseted, narcissistic boredom. 'Strangely enough,' he wrote in *A New Song for the Lord*, 'people from the dominant nations are in no way happy with their type of freedom and power; they feel that they are dependent on anonymous structures that take their breath away – and this even in those places where the form of government assures the greatest possible freedom. Paradoxically, the cry for liberation, for a new exodus into the land of true freedom, sounds particularly loudly among those who have more possessions and mobility at their disposal than we could ever have imagined before.'

'Why', he asked, 'do people take refuge in drugs?' His explanation: 'Because the life that presents itself to them is in reality too shallow, too deficient, too empty. After all the pleasures, all the emancipations, and all the hopes they have pinned to it, there remains a "much-too-little".'

What is often missed by the Church in its attempts to dissuade the faithful from the secular-materialist path is the benefit of telling people how, apart from, as it were, offering an insurance policy on eternity, the Christian message can make their earthly lives better. The antidote to boredom is truth, which is both the Word of Scripture and, more, the Person of Jesus. But, whereas truth is an absolute value, it cannot live if it is not visible in the actuality of people's lives.

We all of us are driven by human passions, instincts, appetites, which have the paradoxical capacity to gratify us with a little of what we desire and destroy us with a little more. John Paul II, echoing Father Luigi Giussani, wrote about such impulses as symptoms of an 'echo of Heaven' within us. Both men remind us that the pursuit of these ideals in the world of the material is doomed to failure and frustration. There is no line at which satisfaction is achieved, but only an endless search for the echo in a confusion of sound and sensation.

The only way of avoiding this contradiction is to seek the echo where it exists: in the soul, in the pursuit of the wholeness from which human dignity flows. This is both the blueprint for happiness and the meaning of morality. 'The primordial human impulse', wrote Joseph Ratzinger, 'that no one can deny and which, ultimately, no one can oppose, is the desire for happiness, to have a fulfilled, completed life.' And moral action, he stressed, is not possible in a unilateral, autonomous way, but develops out of an encounter with God, the knowledge of His truth, and the experiencing of His love. This sounds like something we've heard before, but has about it a new clarity: God is vital for me, my identity and my destiny, and rules exist to save me from errors that will destroy my happiness. It took me fifty years of failure before I began to see this as a possibility in the fog of my existence.

Imagine a combination of the Dublin Horse Show, the Rose of Tralee, the Fianna Fáil Ard Fheis and the Galway Races – with God at the centre of it. An implausible combination, certainly. But this is a reasonably evocative description of the annual Rimini Meeting, which I attended for the first time in 2006 as an invited speaker. Organized by Communion and Liberation, the event is at once incongruous and hugely uplifting for someone reared in the dark shadow of the Irish Church.

Rimini is the Brighton of Italy's Adriatic coast, mostly dedicated to the pursuit of the gods of summer: sun, sand and sea. But every August for the past 28 years, a different reality has lain alongside the basting bodies on the beaches. CL was founded over 50 years ago by Father Luigi Giussani, with his exhilarating sense of the breadth and meaning of faith, and the Meeting is now the organization's most visible public engagement. The Meeting takes place in a gigantic exhibition centre with more than a dozen different spaces. Every year, some 700,000 people, mostly young adults, come from all over the world to this extraordinary festival of faith, commerce, culture, art and science. Several thousand Italian CL members run the festival on a voluntary basis, many travelling long distances and paying their own way.

The theme of the 2006 Meeting was intriguing if long-winded: 'Reason is the need for the Infinite and culminates in the longing and the presentiment that this Infinite be manifested.' Flagship exhibitions on the Milky Way, the Benedictines and the poet Dante were intertwined with debates about everything from Creationism and Darwinism to dieting – some 200 events over seven days.

For someone raised in a version of Catholicism which looks askance at much of reality – especially modern reality – it was at first quite shocking to encounter the incongruous juxtaposition of faith and marketplace. This reflects Father Giussani's insistence that religion 'proposes to man a question regarding everything he does, and thus becomes a much broader point of view than any other'.

Giussani had founded a group called Gioventu Studentesca (Student Youth) aka GS, in 1954, which became CL. On a train journey to the Adriatic coast from Milan, where he was lecturing at the Seminary of Venegono, he had encountered a group of Catholic students and fallen into conversation with them. He was shocked to discover how little they knew of the faith they'd been brought up in. It struck him that, despite the prevailing sense that Italian Catholicism remained strong and deeply rooted, Catholic teaching had been woefully inadequate in equipping these young people for a secular world, or in conveying to them the content of the Christian message. The idea that Catholicism remained healthy, he wrote in *The Journey to the Truth is an Experience*, 'was founded on a strength of the past, and expressed itself on one hand through mass participation in Catholic worship, and on the other – paradoxically – through a strictly political power, very much exploited from the ecclesial point of view'. A resonant description for anyone brought up in the Irish Catholic Church.

Giussani established GS with a view to re-establishing a Christian witness in the Italian education system – to, as he put it, relaunch 'the announcement of Christianity as a present event of human interest and suitable for anyone who does not want to renounce the fulfillment of his or her hopes and expectations, as well as the use, without diminishment, of the gift of reason'. Running through Giussani's many books and teachings is a call for the integration of faith with reality and reason. 'Separating heaven from earth', he wrote in *The Risk of Education*, 'is a crime.' Christianity, he insists, is 'God on earth', an event in history rather than an idea. Jesus exists not as story or metaphor but in the realm of fact. Giussani challenges the assumption that faith and reason follow parallel lines, insisting that they are one. Faith exalts rationality because it answers the cry of the human heart for truth, beauty, justice and love. Faith and reason are one because the human longing for perfection has but one answer: God – our identity and our destiny. There are no questions, says Giussani, without answers. Faith is the highest form of rationality because happiness is synonymous with eternity. To speak of God is the most rational thing in the world.

Giussani's exhilarating vision centres on the valorization of personal experience, on the veneration of tradition combined with a wariness towards traditionalism, and on an elevated sense of what freedom means. In his words there is a challenge to both traditional piety and modern secularism. Unless God is relevant to my life and my experience, he tells me, He has no meaning. But without Him, there is no meaning at all. Religion, says Giussani, is not about morals, but about the fact that God is what defines humanity. Moralism, he states starkly, is idolatry. We require a new approach, combining an awareness of absolute truth with openness towards the shifting nuance of this truth in a changing world.

We often think of the decline of faith as resulting from the hubris arising from increasing knowledge, but this is just half the story. Faith has been isolated from life by both our growing cleverality and a tendency towards over-simplification which insults the burgeoning intelligence of the young. Father Giussani offers a way back. Citing Dante, Shakespeare, Dostoyevsky, Kafka, Kerouac, Solzhenitsyn, Mozart, Leopardi, and a hundred other artists, writers and thinkers, he suggests an alternative to the arid conflict between tradition and modernity, a new way of seeing the moment-to-moment integration of abiding truth with the imperative of the new. If Christianity has a future, this is it. If Ireland has a future, this, too, may well be it.